THE BRAIN WORKS

99 Shades of Play

Seductive Crossword Puzzles That Will Keep You Tied Up for Hours

Myles Mellor

SELLERS
PUBLISHING

Published by Sellers Publishing, Inc.
Copyright © 2013 Sellers Publishing Inc.
Text and puzzles copyright © 2013 Myles Mellor
All rights reserved.

Sellers Publishing, Inc.
161 John Roberts Road, South Portland, Maine 04106
Visit our Web site: www.sellerspublishing.com
E-mail: rsp@rsvp.com

ISBN 13: 978-1-4162-0920-1

Designed by George Corsillo/Design Monsters

10 9 8 7 6 5 4 3 2

Printed and bound in the United States of America.

THE BRAIN WORKS

99 Shades of Play

CROSSWORD PUZZLES

Across

1 How to tie someone up?
5 Show _____
8 Business grad, abbr.
11 Airport pickup
12 _____ dancer
13 Priest's robe
14 Leprechaun's land
15 A Great Lake
16 Bawl
17 Meat-and-cheese store
18 Code of life, abbr.
19 Edge
20 Made ready to dominate
23 Animal park
24 Fishing gear
25 Spheres
27 Ethereal
28 Home of the brave
30 Before, for Wordsworth
31 Beats per minute
36 Out of control . . .
37 Underhanded
38 Clique
40 The greatest boxer
41 Water carrier
42 _____-European
43 That's _____negotiable!
44 Nonchalance
45 Stash away
46 Basis of some divisions
47 False show
48 Kind of hall

Down

1 Took off
2 Buenos _____
3 Say cheese!
4 Bartender's supply
5 Third-largest island in the world
6 Homer's story
7 Last letter
8 Stonework
9 Fair
10 "The Sound of Music" figure
12 Spanish Peters
19 2:00 or 3:00
21 Member of an Asian republic
22 "Don't use that word" sound
25 Iridescent
26 Tear apart
27 A knitting pattern with diamond shapes
28 Bantu language
29 Postscript
30 Enroll for service
32 Sir _____ Newton
33 Someone prejudiced against the elderly
34 Pound piece
35 Provide with a permanent fund
39 Women's evening wear
41 Princess's woe

Across

1 Steeped beverage
4 Emission that's bad for the environment, abbr.
7 Vocal piece
11 Edward's nickname
12 Copacabana site
13 Twosome
14 Grab him in the elevator, perhaps
17 Currently interesting
18 Hygiene action
21 Humorous animal?
24 Conquered in an argument, e.g.
25 Pilot
27 More in Spanish
28 Medical tests
29 Colo. neighbor, abbr.
31 Horse
33 He is the _____!
34 Red Sea borderer
35 Test or analyze
37 Draw him in
40 Shows impatience with the dom
45 Demonic
46 Colorado Native American tribe
47 Meadow
48 June honorees
49 The Med., for one
50 _____ out a living

Down

1 Used to blow things up, abbr.
2 "Lo, How a Rose _____ Blooming"
3 Inner shrines in ancient temples
4 Whip handle
5 Pacific island nation
6 Formulating linguistically
7 Computer term
8 Cheerleader cheer
9 King George _____
10 Escort's offering
15 Freight weight
16 People of southern Mexico
18 Welsh valley
19 Consisting of rich soil
20 Come to pass
22 Forbidden things
23 Boxing site
25 Mediterranean plant
26 Transport
28 Proofreading marks
30 Ottoman governor
32 Parts of backs
35 Big club
36 Sauveness
38 Network of nerves
39 Surface
40 Heart color
41 Reproductive cells
42 "Keep a _____ on it!"
43 Comic character comment
44 Envelope that comes back, abbr.

#2

1 2 3 4 5 6 7 8 9 10
11 12 13
14 15 16
17
18 19 20 21 22 23
24 25 26
27 28 29 30
31 32 33
34 35 36
37 38 39
40 41 42 43 44
45 46 47
48 49 50

Across

1 Clayey soil
5 Human simulator
8 After-school social, abbr.
11 Nautical direction
12 A sparkling wine
13 Jogged
14 Old Italian coin
15 Quality
16 Jedi, first name
17 Skier's aid
18 Sound unit
19 Touch-down time, perhaps, abbr.
20 Cupid's other persona
24 Moniker
25 Respond
26 Get through to
30 Needle
31 Representative
32 Visited
34 All hearts on the poker table
39 Had a salmon bagel
40 D-day participants, abbr.
41 Capitol votes
43 Turkish title
44 South American Indian
45 Insect stage
46 The other woman
47 _____ of the thighs
48 Desktop dominator
49 He wanted a piece of it
50 _____ in his kiss
51 Lake that contains a monster

Down

1 Fountain order
2 Accused's need
3 Showed over
4 Discern
5 Rotten apple
6 Convex molding
7 Road cover
8 Taking on different forms
9 Trademark for a pepper sauce
10 Blackbird
12 Hooded snake
19 Garden with a snake
21 _____ alcohol
22 Accent
23 It's often sloppy
26 Thing, legally
27 Coops up
28 Online players
29 Nucleus
32 Middle-ear bone
33 Append
35 Blow one's top
36 Let her go
37 Bearnaise, e.g.
38 Some needles
42 Not with
43 Eureka!
44 Japanese-food fish

99 Shades of Play

Across

1 Possessive form
4 Be incorrect
7 Knife handle
11 Little one
12 Lament
13 Start to operative
14 Dom assertion of nastiness
17 Attack verbally, S&M style
18 Make-up present
21 Earlier style
25 Forelimb
26 Multitude
30 Moody
31 Roman 3
32 Country bumpkin
34 It's stranded, abbr.
35 Fishing tool (var.)
37 Kind of blocker
38 What little blip became
39 Contract stipulated 7 hours
41 Best white and lacy
43 Otalgia
47 Saint-Exupéry novel, "The _____"
52 Discomfort
53 Classic opener
54 Boat, for short
55 Miller, for one
56 Recipe measurement, abbr.
57 Generation

Down

1 _____ be nice if . . .
2 Additionally
3 Commemorative marker
4 Seabirds
5 Baseball Hall of Famer, Babe
6 Completely fix
7 Traced
8 _____ seed
9 U.S. government agency, abbr.
10 Water tester
15 Prone to cheekiness
16 Possessive
18 Downpours
19 Bay window
20 Hit hard
22 Upper body
23 Chatter
24 Ape
27 Chuck
28 _____ out a living
29 Not just behind the ears . . .
33 Police club
36 Almost fall
40 Homeboy
42 Ergo
44 Monthly check
45 Mimics
46 Field yield
47 Retriever, for short
48 Break the _____
49 Sentence starter
50 One for the road
51 Tampa airport abbreviation

Across

1 It may be easily bruised
4 Make up one's mind
7 Place for a mani
10 Stellar phenomenon
12 Cab fee
13 Bit in a horse's mouth
14 Greek consonants
15 Related
16 Casino cube
17 Play, in a way
19 Combat
20 "I Put a Spell on You" singer
24 Keen insight
25 Platinum bracelet locale
29 Punishment equipment
30 Fortune-teller's card
33 Slippery fish
34 Where you might find a
   sub often, on her _____
36 Cousin of an ostrich
37 Parents
38 Brilliance in bed
41 Milk-soaked bread
43 Mathematician
44 Address to the dom
45 Deft
46 "Wow!"
50 An end to sad
51 For fear that
52 Open wide
53 Possessive thou
54 Rocks at the bar
55 The Mediterranean, for one

Down

1 Compass dir., abbr.
2 Obtained
3 Fertility-clinic stock
4 Jute fiber
5 Top-notch
6 Jack's inferior
7 Flavored water
8 Twosome
9 Wolfed down
11 NE India state
12 Breakfast fare
18 Vampire fly
19 Cyst
20 Police informer, in London
21 Object of worship
22 Hosiery shade
23 Character
26 French military cap
27 Ranch lands
28 Additionally
31 Drive back
32 Ham-and-egg dish
35 Medium-like perception, abbr.
39 Levantine three-master
40 Three in poker
41 "Phooey!"
42 Military group
44 Perch
45 "Love Story" actress
47 Empty talk
48 Overwhelming
   admiration
49 Kind of testing, abbr.

Across

1 Fizzles out
5 Cosmetic mogul middle name
8 Oriental tie
11 Dreadful
12 Chemical ending
13 Brows might do this
14 Submissive position
17 Back of the boat
18 Get the picture
19 Golden Rule word
21 Household urges
24 Chimney channel
25 Times at 12
29 Make a move
30 Fussbudget
31 Lingerie
32 Gave a blow-by-blow
34 Dress and scarf color
35 Certain weaves
36 Maintain
37 Electricity attraction
39 Sun in Spanish
40 Per contract, _____ obedience
47 Drudge
48 "_____ we there yet?"
49 Something to spin
50 Sloppy digs
51 Bow wood
52 Fully fit

Down

1 "Silent Spring" subject, abbr.
2 Third guy with the same name
3 Before of yore
4 Calm
5 Saved
6 Black tropical bird with long tail
7 Intense desires
8 John Lennon's wife
9 Took the bait
10 "_____ magic!"
13 Work, as dough
15 Tabloid topic, abbr.
16 Jazzman G
19 Stomach woe
20 Like some candy bars
22 Triangular end of a building
23 Pancake topping
24 Rage
25 Valueless
26 Poem of praise
27 Uneven
28 "Casablanca" pianist
30 Wild animal
33 Big home-run hitter
34 Ball game
36 Really big goldfish
38 6-June-44
39 Healthy pot
40 Emotional highs
41 Misty May obstacle
42 Playing hard to get
43 Hotness under the collar
44 Catch red-handed
45 Nothing's opposite
46 Actor, Marvin

6

Across

1 Bump
4 Can be Dutch
7 Jasmine, for one
11 Bring into play
12 Stop running, of an engine
13 Honey
14 Musician used in the Red Room
17 A food fish
18 Dixie drink
21 Metals
24 _____ grid, playroom feature
25 Part of a cricketing metaphor
26 Charity-auction offer
27 Macho dude
29 Till bill
31 Shocked
33 At another time
34 Clubbing wear
35 English city
36 Crowd-_____
39 Inner goddess, aka
44 Edible pod of the south
45 Tom Clancy subject, for short
46 Buddy (sl.)
47 Conquer
48 Musical gift
49 Objective

Down

1 Stick (out)
2 Fire remains
3 Recommence
4 Dutch cheese
5 Speech problem
6 Multicellular animals
7 Face shape
8 Eighth Arabic letter
9 Kimono belt
10 Hi-_____ file
15 Hair
16 Negatively charged atom
18 Triangular sail
19 Dickens's Heep
20 Hunting cabin
22 Copy
23 Council
25 World time zone, abbr.
27 Cry for hunting dogs
28 Inner core
30 Naval rank, abbr.
32 Old-time jazz fan
33 An organism that is unable to live without air
35 Aloha gift
37 Mt. Everest's land
38 Leave a mark
39 Break down
40 Island strings
41 Bathing-suit part
42 Roman container
43 Sward

7

Across

1 Provoke
5 One of the finest
8 Govt. regulator, abbr.
11 Deft
12 Las Vegas dancer accessory
13 Shake a _____!
14 Ready-to-eat-you look
17 Atwitter, with "up"
18 Foolish
19 Stout
21 Oakland baseball players
22 Aphrodisiac seafood
26 Sub holder
30 Certain neckline
31 Increase, with "up"
33 Billionaire has a big one
34 Tall story
36 Deodorant type
39 _____-Man (comic-book character)
41 Windswept spot
42 Mixer
46 Expression of disgust
50 Vanilla sex symbol
52 Do it on the beach at Cannes
53 British poet, Hughes
54 Monies borrowed
55 DC time setting, abbr.
56 Day divs., abbr.
57 Small amphibians

Down

1 Stare (at)
2 Mitch Miller's instrument
3 Compatriot
4 Overpower
5 TV network
6 Bedroom sounds
7 Noodles
8 Stomach motion
9 Kosher-style store
10 Wrinkled
15 Lounge
16 Rumple
20 Muff
22 Some ducts carry them
23 The end is not _____
24 Lay
25 Can be open or choppy
27 Thing, legally
28 Back when
29 Campaigner, for short
32 Dog doc
35 With it
37 Drift
38 Prediction
40 Ground
42 Where visitors count
43 Wood sorrels
44 Change component
45 Sinister look
47 Fiddler's place
48 Pesky insect
49 Female lobsters
51 Personals, e.g.

8

Across

1 Encouragement
5 Tooth crowns
9 Meat jelly
11 Old Russian governing body
13 Billionaire interview reaction
16 Risk
17 Ontario natives
18 Take out
19 Insect-eating lizard
21 Billionaire's home
25 Like sheets and good lettuce
30 Poet's Muse
31 A real doll!
32 Drive away
33 Toyota pickup
34 Dislike, and then some
37 Experienced
41 Essence
42 Data-processing unit, abbr.
45 Pauses in the action
48 Make up
49 Clean the slate
50 Pepper's partner
51 Walked (on)

Down

1 Long for
2 Computerphile
3 Active
4 Subject of "Philadelphia," abbr.
5 Scare a sub
6 Insatiable
7 Hummus holder

8 Branch
10 Popular drink
11 Pipe part
12 Everyday article
14 Longing
15 Green color
20 True
21 Pay-_____-view
22 Nirvana song "Come as You __"
23 Drink from a dish
24 Had a good meal
26 Campaign
27 _____ be good if
28 "Dear" one
29 Circular veggie
33 Aaron Spelling's daughter
35 Thai currency
36 Exclamation of surprise
37 Federal investigators, abbr.
38 Seabirds
39 Bulgarian coins
40 East Asian weight
42 Singe
43 Tijuana coin
44 Like hand-me-downs
46 Big blast maker, abbr.
47 Computer monitor, abbr.

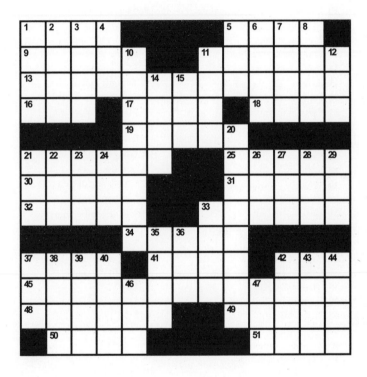

9

Across

1 The Big Apple, abbr.
4 Miss the mark
7 Constrictor
10 Paddle
11 In addition
12 Infinity, almost
13 Drop-dead gorgeous
16 Half a Latin dance
17 Article
18 Detestation
21 Quartet member
24 European birds
25 Cannes beach item
27 Mythical bird
28 Edible flower bulbs
29 "Much __ About Nothing," Shakespeare
31 Rock formation
33 Mideast chief (var.)
34 Evidence
35 More clairvoyant
36 Grand _____, Nova Scotia
37 Charge carrier
38 It might hold a sub
43 Wood furniture
44 _____ the line
45 Repeats 5 times for an Abba song
46 Coin of Burma
47 _____ kitten
48 Pesticide, for short

Down

1 Vetoes
2 Swerve off course
3 Early-spring bloomer
4 Sicilian volcano
5 Scrape
6 Potato, for one
7 Pepper plants
8 _____ and aah
9 To some extent
14 Law man
15 Flightless birds
18 It precedes "The land of the free"
19 Go limp
20 Sustain
22 Consisting of rich soil
23 Golden _____
25 Makes ideal
26 Green light
28 Contempt
30 U of M basketball coach, Johnny
32 Kansas city
33 Poem by Virgil
35 Favoring
37 Goat
38 Coxcomb
39 Jamie Foxx's legend
40 Shed item
41 Sum up
42 Morse-code symbol

Across

1 Opinion
4 Clairvoyant's gift
7 Type of reseller, for short
10 Hit the books
12 Aware of
13 Investment vehicle
14 Site of the Taj Mahal
15 Small cave
16 Group of former Soviet republics, abbr.
17 Aqua- _____
18 Encircle
19 _____ baby!
20 Ardor in full flower?
23 Pay dirt
24 Golden rule preposition
25 Carpentry wedges
28 Redwoods, e.g.
29 Subtle glow
30 Lookout point
31 Locked lips
37 "The Cat in the _____"
38 Slashed in two
39 Blemishes
40 Web site abbreviation
41 Clickable image
42 Alcoholic drink
43 Trumped-up story
44 Hustles
45 Hollywood favorite
46 Bottom (sl.)
47 Deplete
48 Family address

Down

1 Harshly criticize
2 Dispute
3 Tall tales
4 Cover up
5 Foot rest
6 Stew mix
7 French noble
8 Melodic compositions
9 Bold
11 Wise men
12 Flirtatious viewers
21 Believers in love, eventually
22 Still alone
25 Overland expeditions
26 Goes very fast
27 E.U. member
28 Slot machine items
30 Crowd
32 Drink served with marshmallows
33 "Tobermory" writer
34 Heaps
35 Concluding stanza
36 Wheels' partner
37 Polynesian dance

Across

1 Empty spaces
5 Bacon kin
8 Specify
12 Distinctive style
13 Roth, maybe, abbr.
14 Hero
15 Release from a nasty hanging
18 Prayer
19 Hurried
22 Elephantine
26 Lazily
27 Salty area
29 Roman 7
30 Motel
31 Sloppy eater
33 Amazing adventure
36 Wizard
37 Asian capital
38 Reputation
39 Stone artifact
42 $100,000
49 Popular cookie
50 Kind of instinct
51 Barely adequate
52 Nuisance
53 Tux followers
54 Water carrier

Down

1 Salon goo
2 Honey Brown
3 One way to stand
4 Exclusive
5 Old stereo system

6 Aesthetic fields
7 Reddish brown
8 U.S. service agency, abbr.
9 Stir
10 Cow murmur
11 Deer
16 Cook an egg
17 Writer Bagnold
19 Immune-system virus, abbr.
20 Bye-bye
21 Trombone moving piece
23 High marks in exams
24 China and India divider
25 Boreal forest
27 Take out of position
28 Compass direction, abbr.
32 Threaten, with at
34 Hi!
35 Hard fat
36 The ransom plot, for one
38 And so forth, abbr.
40 Praise
41 Obsessed with
42 Smart dresser
43 Displeasure
44 Thing, legally
45 A drunk
46 Small amount
47 Heretofore, for a poet
48 Ever, to Keats

99 Shades of Play

Across

1 Alternative to steps
5 Chop off
8 L.A. cloud
12 Reed instrument
13 Big goon
14 Window section
15 Stun, romantically
17 Single item
18 Initial entry into billionaire's office
20 Essential oil from flowers
23 Boundary
24 Farm soil
25 Revolution
27 Soda _____
28 Greek Island
29 "That feels good!"
32 Because of
33 Saab, for one
34 Rancher's concern
35 Honeydew, e.g.
36 Suspicious hardware-store purchase
39 Palestinian city
40 Baby related
44 Head or night starter
45 Jazzman
46 Centers of activity
47 _____ radio
48 Time span
49 Green-_____ monster

Down

1 Hold up
2 Blood system, abbr.
3 Trim the lawn
4 Battle in the American Revolution
5 Volcanologist's study
6 Newspaper page
7 Lovely!
8 Type of bush
9 Minister's home
10 Sleep _____
11 Catch
16 Byron's over
19 Not playing
20 European peak
21 Very
22 Listening device
25 Believability
26 "Are we there _____?"
28 Salon product
29 Feel awful
30 Hubbub
31 Egg layer
32 Get off a ship
33 Kind of value
34 Eye color
35 Game pieces
36 A sparkling wine
37 Race
38 Itty bit
39 Understood
41 Miniature
42 Deck card
43 Top of a pot

#13

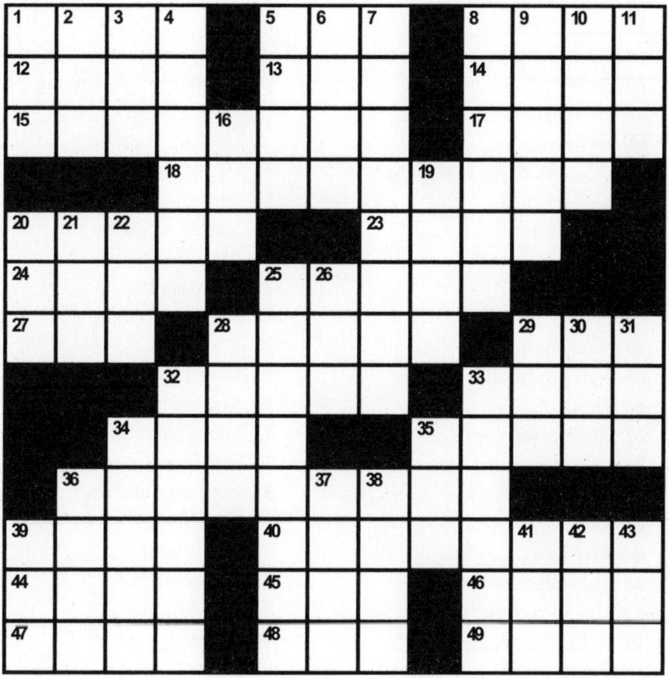
1 2 3 4 5 6 7 8 9 10 11
12 13 14
15 16 17
18 19
20 21 22 23
24 25 26
27 28 29 30 31
32 33
34 35
36 37 38
39 40 41 42 43
44 45 46
47 48 49

99 Shades of Play

Across

1 Betting data
5 Eastern path
8 Moistens
12 King in India
13 "_____ Together Now"
14 Declare frankly
15 Adjust
16 Young goat
17 Beginner
18 One way to get him going
21 Solitary man
22 Do poorly
23 Hauls with tackle
24 Surgical tool
28 Horse feed
29 Have remorse for
30 TV show to make out to
34 Think
37 Author, Harper
38 Drug-traffic investigator
39 Sexy and studlike
43 Tilt
44 Recognize
45 Cable alternative
48 Do _____ others
49 Robinson or Jones
50 Bounce back
51 Supervisor
52 Drunkard
53 Action

Down

1 Copper or bronze
2 Head of the family
3 Northern African country
4 Glossy fabrics
5 "Any _____?"
6 Dismounted
7 Dated
8 Turkey skin
9 The dark force
10 Musician Amos
11 Barter
19 Start of a giggle
20 An _____ ball
21 Hang around
23 Exchange blows
25 _____ makes perfect!
26 Camera setting
27 Maiden name
31 South American plains
32 Startled cry
33 California shakes
34 Swallow
35 Code word
36 Undercut
39 Bungle
40 Gambling mecca
41 Chow
42 Claudius's successor
46 Lady under discussion
47 Mortar trough

Across

1 Chain to the bed
5 Candy holder
8 Liberal _____
12 Style of molding
13 According to
14 Chicken was a preferred one in the hospital
15 Contents of Pandora's box
16 Software program
17 Epic story
18 Hopping-mad submissive
21 Exist
22 PC key
23 Horse handler
26 Magnetic-field densities
30 Get your ducks all in a _____!
31 Self-image
32 Joke subject
36 Host
39 Postapartheid org., abbr.
40 Word of success
41 Fallen madly, a la Beyoncé
46 Pigtail components
48 Endless time
49 Lingual
50 Fliers' org., abbr.
51 Prison shot
52 Persuade
53 Catty remark
54 Dummy
55 Works in the garden

Down

1 Arrange hair
2 Tangelo type
3 Was aware of his touch
4 Merry
5 Make noisy bird talk
6 Hand-cream ingredient
7 Door-knock sound
8 Things to show off
9 Highway
10 Yank
11 Springs area
19 Basic metal
20 French for island
23 Christmas-tree decor
24 Musical "G"
25 Deuce
27 Neck surround
28 "Give it _____!"
29 Scion
33 Thin
34 Kind of evidence, abbr.
35 Skin problem
36 Fabrications
37 Even, old way
38 Waterproof overshoe
41 "Bye"
42 Addressing two or more people in slang
43 Sandwich cookie
44 Low-lying area
45 Corner pieces
46 Guy
47 Virtuoso

#15

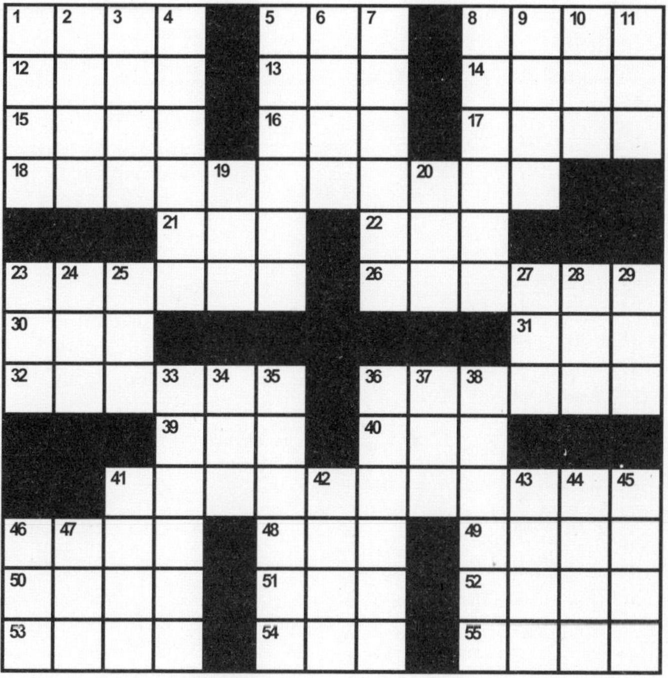

Across

1 Like some columns
5 Smashed
8 Like some beds
12 Carpet layer's calculation
13 Summer in Paris
14 Erelong
15 Smooch to say I'm sorry
18 Catch sight of
19 Poisonous fruit
22 Soon to be insects
26 Card game
30 Nuisance
31 Past
32 Customs
34 Ham holder
35 Hinged device
37 Mediterranean flower
39 "Sesame Street" character
41 Keen
42 The act of deleting
46 Mediterranean flower smell
52 The good life
53 It may be loaded
54 Make public
55 Touch-down times, abbr.
56 Hot tub
57 Just a smidgen

Down

1 Dunce
2 Country-club figure
3 Ballad ending
4 Knife
5 First name in jeans
6 Tabloid twosome
7 Occasional worker
8 All part of looking cute
9 "Gimme _____!" (start of an Iowa State cheer)
10 Old computer operating system, abbr.
11 Lowest commissioned officer, abbr.
16 Small-intestine section
17 Great perception, abbr.
19 Obviously surprised
20 Stogie
21 Famous
23 Hidden
24 In the past
25 Inscribed pillar
27 Extinct flightless bird
28 The infamous Robinson's intro
29 "Sure"
33 River through Chad
36 Feudal sovereigns
38 Butterfly wing's eyes
40 Baseball stat., abbr.
43 Sex _____
44 Remove a tag
45 Eye section
46 Quilting party
47 Breakfast grain
48 Home of the brave, abbr.
49 Zodiac sign
50 Dom's most frequent order
51 Rap-sheet letters, abbr.

16

Across

1 Sketched
5 Prime example of stubbornness
8 Poetic foot
12 Distinctive air
13 Popular music category
14 Madison Avenue award
15 After being chased reaction
18 Update from the rickshaw
19 Cannes is on one
22 Cirque de Soleil employees
26 NHL great
27 "Back in the _____"
30 Plaything the billionaire is no good at
31 Time of one's life
32 Reverent
34 "Lord of the Rings" evil warrior
35 Strong taste
37 Eyesore
38 Gobbled up
39 Chant
41 Honey badger
43 Leather from a goat
46 Sade's "Your Love Is King"
52 Scent
53 Southwest native
54 Computer image
55 Departed
56 Small gull
57 Diamond, e.g.

Down

1 Lentil sauce
2 Parisian way
3 .0000001 joule
4 Narrow-waisted stingers
5 Parched
6 Japanese liquor
7 Broad range
8 Early-day refrigerator
9 The works
10 "Thanks a _____!"
11 Crowd disapproval sound
16 Abate
17 Glass container
19 Raccoon relative
20 Piped instrument
21 Contraction
23 Subsurface war vessel
24 La _____ County, Indiana
25 Surpass
28 Percussion instrument
29 Paltry amount
33 Shoot
36 Racing vehicle
40 Zippo
42 Tomfoolery
44 Web location
45 Was aware of
46 Dispute
47 Hymn
48 Over there
49 Edible tuber
50 Fish-fowl connection
51 Call off

Across

1 Expert
4 Andes' kin
7 Protect
11 Russian Parliament earlier
13 Plaintive cry
14 Horsefly
15 Large dirigible
17 Pearl Mosque site
18 Your wish _____
20 Lets go
22 Indian coin
23 Had a granola
24 S. American tubers
26 Pompous fool
27 Ecological community
28 _____ wolf
31 One of Chekhov's "Three Sisters"
32 _____ and cry
33 Knitted present
36 Boss, in Swahili
38 Avoid being forthright with billionaire
41 O. Henry's "The Gift of the _____"
42 When the dom feels wronged, he will take _____s
45 Plane arrival times, abbr.
46 Fail to obey the dom
47 Wedding throwaway
48 Used to be
49 Period in time
50 It's a mess

Down

1 Woodworker's tool
2 Billiards stick or a signal
3 Domains
4 Deftly
5 Not of the cloth
6 View from the new house
7 Little rascal
8 Water slime
9 Captain Nemo's creator
10 Quaint outburst
12 Cathedral recess
16 Expressions of hesitation
19 Ponder
20 Civil-aviation controllers, abbr.
21 _____ a good plan!
24 Kind of furnace
25 Toothed wheel
27 Low-quality diamond
28 Car body
29 Bleed
30 Word of success
33 Figure _____
34 Humidor item
35 Develop
36 Dental-drill part
37 Small dam
38 Duck breed
39 "Que _____," Doris Day song
40 Nimble
43 Behave
44 Grazing land

#18

1
2
3
4
5
6
7
8
9
10
11
12
13
14
15
16
17
18
19
20
21
22
23
24
25
26
27
28
29
30
31
32
33
34
35
36
37
38
39
40
41
42
43
44
45
46
47
48
49
50

99 Shades of Play

Across

1 Sprite, for one
5 Venus or Mars
8 Trigonometry expression, abbr.
12 Gem cut
13 Cone-producing tree
14 Reputation
15 Versailles nightmare locale
18 Public-transportation staging area
19 Arise
22 Coagulates
25 Annoyance word
26 Round
28 Noise
29 Black _____ event
30 Hard limits are _____ negotiable
32 Small tiles
35 Father
36 Oyster gem
37 Billonaire's instrument, when young
38 Oats container
41 Face of the really offended
47 Chime
48 Beat badly in the playroom
49 Gaelic language
50 Seattle, for one
51 Frequently, to Keats
52 Prerequisite

Down

1 Musical-scale note
2 Female reproductive cells
3 Eighth Arabic letter
4 Not quite
5 Rubs out
6 Rolls around the edge
7 Knickerbockers, informally
8 Inertia
9 Tumult
10 Easter preceder
11 Time segments, abbr.
16 Your and my
17 Dom or sub, e.g.
19 Abnormal
20 Hamper
21 Dugout
23 Fungal skin disease
24 Treat with disdain
26 Now that's a real heel
27 Flick
31 Classic opener
33 Without risk
34 Mars, to the Greeks
35 Real mess
37 Friend
39 Unhearing
40 Crooked
41 U.K. TV
42 Flower garland
43 Final, abbr.
44 Metal
45 Treat shabbily
46 "CSI" star, Danson

99 Shades of Play

Across

1 Romances
5 Playing hard to get
8 Unappealing fruit?
12 Hip bones
13 "We _____ Family"
14 Straight
15 Window ledge
16 Teacher's favorite
17 Sales personnel
18 Keeping him to yourself grammatically
21 Singer, DiFranco
22 Malta, for one
25 Sub meat
28 Over the moon
31 Great time
32 Small guitar, for short
33 "So that's your game!"
35 Give light to
39 Neither's alternative
40 Common bar purchases
41 _____ the line
43 Billionaire's showerhead size
49 Taj Mahal location
52 Rainbow's shape
53 __operative
54 Harmony
55 Sun
56 Little dent
57 Fix, in a way
58 Stretch out
59 Bitch troll and others

Down

1 A lock of hair
2 Assortment
3 Painter's medium
4 Hot dance
5 Pepper plant
6 Mine finds
7 Fictional ape
8 Turmoil
9 "Oh, my!"
10 Place for a sleeping head
11 Possessive pronoun
19 WSW's opposite
20 Itinerary word
23 Brave individual
24 Bounce back, in a way
25 Gentleman
26 Puccini piece
27 Shopping center
29 Glide over white stuff
30 Feeler
34 Connective word
36 It gets handed down
37 America, abbr.
38 Waiting period, seemingly
42 Chopin piece
44 Destroy
45 Understand
46 Computer operating system
47 Teenage problem
48 Christmas drinks
49 Burro
50 Swindle
51 Part of a cell nucleus, abbr.

Across

1 Brilliant fish
5 Mason's burden
8 Femme fatale
12 Piece of glass
13 Word of support
14 Healing shrub
15 Escape from the dom's control
18 Madrigal music
19 Inuit vessel
22 Ancient Italian
26 Life, for one
30 Taro root
31 Postapartheid org., abbr.
32 Bellini heroine
34 Seafood selection
35 U.S. island of the Philippines
37 Holding on, won't let go
39 Nonfiction work
41 _____ and dangerous
42 Feel happiness or joy
46 Sub's answer to "Can you come over at 9?"
52 Storage space
53 Lunched
54 Blackjack
55 Liquify by warmth
56 _____ de plume
57 Listen to

Down

1 Clancy's black _____
2 Sidekick
3 Tropical American cuckoo
4 Cool guy in the '50s
5 Chemistry Nobelist, Otto
6 Court call
7 Painting style
8 Bag
9 "_____ About Eve"
10 Flightless bird
11 Capita beginning
16 Tess was ___ by Alec
17 Mrs. John Lennon
19 Grammar topic
20 Food choices
21 Pizarro's conquest
23 Kind of drive, abbr.
24 Glorify
25 It has _____ (eternity)
27 Discouraging words
28 Credit, abbr.
29 Walking-only bird
33 Primitive calculators
36 Woodchuck
38 Rear
40 Urge
43 She's from Arcadia
44 Director, Preminger
45 Part of a list
46 Doctrine
47 Disapproving expression
48 Chicago's state, abbr.
49 Defendant called John
50 Consumption
51 Doctor's degree, abbr.

99 Shades of Play

Across

1 Put to _____
4 Neon, e.g.
7 Small wound
11 Religious denomination
13 Earlier
14 Gait between walk and canter
15 Teen's woe, with heart
16 Flat hat
17 _____ and every
18 Don't let these things roll around in the wrong place!
21 To _____ for
22 Genetic info carrier, abbr.
23 Wine fave
27 To be, in old Rome
31 Fla. neighbor, abbr.
32 Necklace stone
34 Squealer
35 Galileo's birthplace
37 Becoming shallow
39 Raise a stink
41 Plate
42 Screwed up in his thinking
47 Skirt or BMW
48 Potash
49 Equipment
51 Alliance
52 Order of corn
53 A snap
54 Russian tennis star, first name
55 Cow or sow
56 Charge

Down

1 America's letters
2 Parts of a min., abbr.
3 Australian anteaters
4 Entry point
5 Seaweed gelatin substitute
6 Hat
7 Commemorative tablets
8 Face-to-face exam
9 Birds of mammoth size
10 Suffix for do and go
12 Purposeful, in grammar
19 Number two
20 Indefinite article
23 Suck dry, as energy
24 Clay, now
25 Fashions again
26 Half a cheerleader cry
28 North American plant with pinkish flowers
29 George Jr. to George Sr.
30 Lay an _____ (mess up)
33 Plaster base
36 Used for treating bruises
38 Feudal lord
40 Thunder's state, abbr.
42 Where firing takes place
43 Privy to
44 Hindu caregiver
45 Bone-dry
46 Emit light
47 Business grad, abbr.
50 Whiskey ingredient

Across

1 Throaty noise
5 "Down under" avian
8 Entreaty
12 Skin-cream additive
13 Panel truck
14 Housing payment
15 After-haircut nickname
18 Bathroom need
19 Obscure
22 Cannes gift
27 Nirvana song "Come as You _____"
28 Albanian coin
30 Pub offerings
31 Ooze
33 Night bird
34 Prefix, half
35 Someone to look up to
36 Minute
37 Central
38 Cambridge grad
40 Beautiful people
42 Mountainous
45 It has several boxes of tricks in it
52 Verse writer
53 Distorted
54 Visit
55 Unattractive
56 Prince, to a king
57 Pianist, Dame Myra

Down

1 Zodiac animal
2 Will Smith title role
3 Cry for help, abbr.
4 Green Italian sauce
5 December 24 and 31
6 Floor protectors
7 Get rid of the belt
8 Experienced
9 Bucharest money
10 One-striper, abbr.
11 Had a Greek yoghurt
16 Hairpiece
17 Rustic locale
19 Elementary
20 Author, Jong
21 Outlaw
23 _____ as a wet hen
24 Varnish resin
25 Send
26 Digression
28 Those uninterested in intellectual matters
29 Madam sheep
32 Explosive letters
39 Performance
40 Idea of oneself
41 Former P.M. of Ireland
43 Haircut
44 Mistress of Charles II
45 PC "brain," abbr.
46 Monopolize
47 Anguillidae
48 Pigs' digs
49 Buck's partner
50 German river
51 Chess end it, abbr.

99 Shades of Play

Across

1 Well-liked president
4 Time-zone basis, abbr.
7 Bikini section
10 Sparkling wine
12 Untrained
13 Perceived
14 _____-steven
15 Rope-a-dope boxer
16 Be jealous of
17 Bad guy, in love
20 Zeppelin intro
21 Has a long bath
24 Cries of pleasure or pain
28 Medieval lady
30 Surprised interjection
31 Weaken
33 Listen here
34 Tempter
37 Wicker or willow
40 Heart_____
42 Battle
43 Inner goddess skating-rink move
48 Breastplate of Zeus
51 Stan who created "Spider-Man"
52 Soprano's song, maybe
53 Bloody
54 Hot air
55 White-handed gibbons
56 Lyric poem
57 USNA grad., abbr.
58 Approval

Down

1 Cold, at Starbucks
2 Intoxicant
3 _____ and anon
4 Relative
5 African country
6 Fire starters
7 He's big in Pittsburgh
8 Accelerate sharply
9 _____ day now
11 It got marked on the honeymoon
13 Stiff hairs
18 Mauna _____ Observatory
19 Reporter's question
22 On bended _____
23 Take a hike!
24 Call for rescue letters
25 Have conversation
26 "Portnoy's Complaint" author
27 Kinsman
29 Time periods, for short
32 Wild
35 Like craft shows
36 Neither rain _____ . . .
38 Self-titled envelope
39 African pen
41 Nonsense
44 Song of triumph
45 Encephalogram
46 Dublin country
47 Glasgow girl
48 Id counterpart
49 Pan, e.g.
50 Pique condition

Across

1 August baby
4 Poorly lit
7 Thick piece
11 Cash machine, abbr.
12 Difficulty
13 Fortune
14 Red Room couch
17 Alluring quality
18 Put to test
21 Transparent
24 Accordingly
25 State clearly
27 Video _____
28 "Forget it!"
29 Owns
31 Lamp type
33 Goldberg variations composer
34 U.S. general
35 Crackers
36 Lettuces
39 Jealousy stimulator
44 Dehydrated
45 Shackle
46 Time from seed
47 Jury member
48 She
49 "_____ what?"

6 Mediterranean country native
7 Ornamental shrub
8 Fib
9 Including the kitchen sink
10 Much-visited location
15 Insidious
16 To the greatest degree
18 And so forth
19 Persian potentates
20 Garden tree
22 Buddhist who has attained Nirvana
23 Strike back
25 Canine's long biters
26 Meadow muncher
28 Score
30 Short
32 Hang around
33 Racketeer
35 Billionaire sibling
37 Soft cheese
38 Still-life subject
39 Venom source
40 Society-page word
41 Bonanza find
42 It's _____
43 _____fangled

Down

1 Genevan water
2 Old verb ending
3 Endings
4 Just the facts, ma'am
5 Same as mentioned

Across

1 Some tributes
5 Bearded beast
8 Propagates
12 Floral arrangement
13 Printed
14 Cozy spot
15 Round, waxed cheese
16 Tide competitor
17 Pirate cry, with there
18 Rueful expletive
21 Wild thing
22 Unhealthy atmosphere
25 Suggest
28 Capelike collar
29 Cross shape
30 Landscaper's grass
31 Vatican vestment
33 Crotchety-dom description
36 China grass
38 Oops
39 "Yes _____!"
40 Won't look at anyone else
45 Place for lox
48 Forest female
49 Wee bit
50 _____ as we speak
51 Squeeze (out)
52 Paint layer
53 Hand over
54 Do-over
55 Aisle leads to it

Down

1 Newspaper page

2 Dumb cluck
3 Genesis twin
4 Logo, for example
5 Roll out the red carpet for
6 Detective
7 Defenseless
8 Get hissy over his control perhaps
9 _____-la-la
10 Try to win a heart
11 Wild blue yonder
19 Stretched out on the bed
20 Get off one's chest
23 Ersatz
24 West African Republic
25 Computer department, abbr.
26 Self-defense spray
27 Cat murmur
28 "Whew!"
30 Baked dessert
32 "Let It _____," Beatles advice
34 Bearlike
35 Wino
36 The girl from Ipanema came from here
37 Herb
39 Shooting sport
41 Pepsi's rival
42 Basketball's destination
43 Airport scheduling-board abbreviations
44 Judge
45 Month, for short
46 Holiday lead-in
47 Made the first move

Across

1 Apply crudely
5 Kooky
8 Dish cooked in a pot
12 Gumbo vegetable
13 Card game
14 Shallow receptacle
15 Bank deposit
16 Get very thin
18 Lost control
20 Desert creature
23 Indigenous
26 Plant served like potato
27 Diamond's site
30 Increase, with "up"
31 Punishment tool
32 Like some symmetry
34 Choler
35 Latch onto
37 Time past
38 Johnson work
39 Clothing line
41 Trig functions
43 Pleasure seeker, like the billionaire
46 Bombast
48 Boast
52 Whoop
53 Solitary
54 Exaggerated talk
55 Wagon part
56 Beatty of "Deliverance"
57 Mystery Nepalese

Down

1 Windows forerunner, abbr.
2 Letters before an alias
3 Jar
4 Symbol of authority
5 Actor, Wilson
6 Woman of distinction
7 Come close
8 They make you stand tall
9 Long-standing activity
10 Dine out
11 Track arrangement
17 Mole org., abbr.
19 Earthen water pot
20 Dog
21 Squirreled-away item
22 Dom's emotion, frequently
24 Cape _____ Island
25 Fencing swords
28 Figure of speech
29 Life story in miniature
33 Take away
36 Retro car
40 Big fuss
42 Restless
44 Prime-time hour
45 Conquered
46 Shag rug
47 Witch's weapon
49 Bar order
50 Select, with "for"
51 Chinese river

99 Shades of Play

Across

1 VW Beetle, for one
5 One of LBJ's beagles
8 Sheltered spot
12 Unappetizing food
13 Need to pay
14 Bitter
15 Dope
16 _____ your engine
17 Rolling rock
18 Soothing classical music
21 Heel and _____
22 Lament
23 Pale tan
26 Rotten apple
30 Dr. Frankenstein's workplace
31 Arriving soon
32 Flew too close to the sun
36 In
39 Cable network
40 A la mode's side
41 It covered up honeymoon marks
48 Isolated
49 Turncoat
50 Can't stand
51 Cold one
52 Mountain or prickly
53 _____ Nicole Smith
54 Guinness and others
55 Nervous
56 Put on

Down

1 Supposing
2 It parallels a radius
3 Good source of protein
4 City near the Douro River
5 Played (around)
6 Cruet
7 Studio effect
8 Given a cash worth
9 Health-giving berry
10 Exist
11 Waxed cheese
19 Very long time
20 As
23 The "greatest" boxer
24 Fond du _____, Wisconsin
25 CEO's degree, abbr.
27 Formerly Tokyo
28 What supports a tooth
29 "Wow!"
33 Doms
34 Bring into play
35 Native-born Israelis
36 Impassiveness
37 Nervous twitch
38 Farm cry
41 Spanish duke
42 Season to be jolly
43 "Trick" joint
44 Impetuous
45 Rural route
46 Sicilian smoker
47 Shred

Across

1 Hole piercers
5 Sharp left or right
8 Sun emission
11 Delicious bar, abbr.
12 Pride
13 Nasty
14 Off-limits (var.)
15 Buffoon
16 Cry over spilled milk
17 Burning with desire
20 Campaigner, for short
21 Musical composition
24 Seafood aphrodisiac
28 Romantic symbol
30 Pizzeria order
31 Poodle's cry
33 Computer letters
34 Cart brake
37 Operations expert
40 Corporate department
42 Confident solver's tool
43 Little-blip detector
48 Coed dwelling area
51 Scoundrel
52 Hang out
53 Times in classifieds
54 Packed away
55 Freedom from stress
56 Roll of dough
57 Pops
58 River herring

Down

1 Deeds
2 Kapow!
3 Western wolf
4 Mold or carve artwork
5 Rings and things
6 Seaweed substance
7 Golf score
8 1959 John Wayne film, "_____ Bravo"
9 Yodeling mountain
10 '70s rock group
13 Fashion
18 Buck's mate
19 Maximum
22 Freshwater fish
23 As a result, in Latin
24 Roman goddess of plenty
25 Barks
26 Some injections
27 Familial comrade
29 "Oz" man
32 Develops from a larva
35 Grads
36 Make sense
38 Attorney's thing
39 Mysterious pieces of wisdom
41 Leash
44 New Zealand tree with hard red wood
45 Salt Lake City state
46 Astronaut's insignia, abbr.
47 Like Easter eggs
48 Morning mist
49 Egg cells
50 One end of the spectrum

99 Shades of Play

Across

1 Aspen conveyer
5 "Silent Spring" subj., abbr.
8 Ball cherries
12 Animal instinct
13 Blow it
14 Religious painting
15 Miss
16 Little white thing
17 Waterproof canvas
18 Interview probe
21 _____ favorite
22 Appetizer
26 Glittering affair
30 Soups
31 Scrap glass
33 In ecstasy
34 Sanctuary
35 People who get things off
their chests
39 Control freaky
44 Quiet
45 "Dee-lish!"
46 Finish off
48 Waiting
49 Gray piece
50 Not deceived by
51 Origin
52 "The Simpsons" character,
Flanders
53 Look of lust

Down

1 Pull on one's heartstrings

2 Military jail
3 Pearl Mosque site
4 Trust
5 Bamboozles
6 Fruit, sometimes
7 Long lock
8 Nibbling sarcastically?
9 United Nations agency
acronym
10 Fate goddesses
11 Econ. indicator, abbr.
19 Hebrew letter
20 Direction indicator
22 Highway radios, abbr.
23 Live
24 Oui's opposite
25 Connected
27 _____ that glitters
28 Moldovan money
29 Kind of card, abbr.
31 Moved around on a billiard
table
32 Former Communist power,
abbr.
36 Stephen King novel
37 Semisynthetic textile
38 Chopin piece
39 Fellow
40 Vacation destination, perhaps
41 Icon
42 Top rated
43 Dietary, in ads
44 HRH part
47 Neither's alternative

99 Shades of Play

Across

1 Madly in love
5 Slow toss
8 Wrinkled-skin fruit
12 Matures
13 Be off base
14 Without ice
15 Makeshift ties
18 Hot-dog container
19 Some like it hot
20 At full throttle
23 Swiftness
26 "Phooey!"
27 Let's go!
29 Wee hour
30 Slept a little
31 Best
33 Hormone secreted from the pancreas
35 Hip joint
36 Island in the Mediterranean
37 Gem mineral
38 Long-eared beast
39 Good times
40 Initial suspicious gut feeling
47 Male chicken
48 Auberge
49 Money in Belgium
50 Roll-call votes
51 Alec was one in "Tess of the D'Urbervilles"
52 Marsh plant

Down

1 Chatter
2 Middle East title
3 Obtain
4 Trash can
5 Rock group, Kings of _____
6 Sphere
7 Lay members of a religious order
8 Restless
9 Gooey stuff
10 Long., opposite, abbr.
11 "_____ showtime!"
16 Hosiery defect
17 Stubble's final phase
20 Stink
21 Freaking out
22 Field of play
24 One-on-one specialist
25 Adhesive
27 Kind of medicine
28 Compact weapon
30 Dared, in Shakespeare
32 Intimate
34 "Shows her" in the playroom
35 Bull's-eye location
37 You can ride one
39 Provide with financing
40 Frigid
41 Bambi's mom
42 Andes plant
43 Cellular stuff, abbr.
44 Color
45 Frequent emotion for the dom
46 Stylish, in the '60s

Across

1 Instructions
5 Will Ferrell character
8 Sensitive
11 Lofty
12 Small bit
13 Italian aloha
14 Next to Europe
15 Unique
16 Muscle woe
17 Suspicious hardware-store purchase
20 Railway, for short
21 Playroom expected response
22 Pond buildup
25 "The father of modern physics"
29 Chinese river
30 Animal's mouth
31 Go off course
32 Incessantly
35 Willow
37 Body soother
38 Calendar square
39 Stomach-jangling insects
44 Skilled stalker
46 Slice of history
47 Chevy hybrid
48 Tart
49 Boundary
50 Traveling
51 ___ Paese cheese
52 Honeymoon water
53 Of sound mind

Down

1 Fraud
2 Tuscan city
3 Auspices
4 Yoga center
5 Black wood
6 Respiratory organ
7 Fine-toothed cutter
8 Chinese staple
9 "I see!"
10 Calamity
13 Blue Grotto site
18 Martinique, for example
19 Have something to complain about
22 Barley beard
23 Baseball's Durocher
24 Tonic go-with
25 Hole
26 Hawaiian headwear
27 Earlier
28 "Catch-22" character
30 They shed
33 Seattle view from new house
34 Small songbird
35 Lummox
36 Forest trees
38 Play making
39 Recipe direction
40 Cleveland's lake
41 Des Moines is its capital
42 Liveliness
43 Eyelid woe
44 Big pooch
45 Hotel sign

32

Across

1 Swindle
5 Sounders' supporter
8 Fortune
11 Highest quality
12 Professional
13 Sub station
14 Mob rule
15 Foolish talk
16 Pea holders
17 Dark side inside
20 Beatles collaborator
21 Needing a shave
24 Egyptian king
28 Pedigree
30 Relief
31 Singer, Starr
33 Special effects, abbr.
34 Gobble down cookies
37 Cannes joyride vehicles
40 Negligible amounts
42 Romanian monetary unit
43 First sign of new baby
48 Ranch newborn
51 Kimono sash
52 English river
53 In a proper manner
54 Masefield play, "The Tragedy of _____"
55 Sounded
56 _____ we done yet?
57 Dyne's cousin
58 Almond and pecan

Down

1 Madras material
2 Mint
3 Unknown writer, abbr.
4 Streak in the sky
5 Journal
6 Type of berry
7 Profundity
8 "Seinfeld" uncle
9 Outmoded
10 "_____ better to have loved . . ."
13 Advanced degree, abbr.
18 Cellular stuff, abbr.
19 City transport
22 Solid foundation
23 He's "smarter than the average bear!"
24 Father figures
25 Drake's ship, "The Golden _____"
26 Shevat follower
27 "The _____" (Uris novel)
29 Appoint starter
32 Shouting
35 Good news on Wall Street
36 J. Edgar's agency, abbr.
38 Driver's location
39 Corrupt
41 "Basic Instinct" star, last name
44 Way to the top
45 Island feast
46 Does not exist
47 Identifies
48 Kind of approval, abbr.
49 Yours and mine
50 Stein contents

Across

1 Doesn't dare oppose the dom
5 It's spotted in casinos
8 _____ him a kiss
12 Square footage
13 Sci-fi gun
14 Irish Ireland
15 _____ tide
16 Coming into view
18 Fashionable panties
20 Pastoral poem
22 Sexy
23 Name
24 In need of a massage
27 A small piece
31 National bird of Australia
32 Model, Campbell
34 Ottoman officer
35 Heroic tale
37 Swamp thing
38 Type of wood
39 _____ behaving badly
41 Area of fertility in a desert
43 Exhibitionist area
47 An era
48 1996 Broadway rock opera
51 Sitter's headache
52 5th is a famous one
53 The Supremes, e.g.
54 Vibe
55 Alkaline liquid
56 Pale

Down

1 Colorless
2 Indignation
3 Fruit-tree destroyer
4 Pontifical
5 Squirrel nest
6 Metrical unit
7 Love and move would constitute one
8 Sires
9 Willingly, old way
10 Eagles by the shore
11 Seriously aroused
17 Girl from Ipamena town
19 Family group
20 The _____ of March
21 Russian Parliament earlier
25 Hometown fair
26 Weed
28 Tavern keepers
29 Jamaican fruit
30 Chesapeake and San Francisco
33 Darling
36 Drink this — live forever
40 Struggling artists _____ out a living
42 It comes from the heart
43 Llama land
44 Sixth month of the Jewish calendar
45 A favorite suit color
46 Elation
47 A good degree, abbr.
49 Fed. agency, abbr.
50 Don't _____ with her emotions!

#34

1
2
3
4
5
6
7
8
9
10
11
12
13
14
15
16
17
18
19
20
21
22
23
24
25
26
27
28
29
30
31
32
33
34
35
36
37
38
39
40
41
42
43
44
45
46
47
48
49
50
51
52
53
54
55
56

Across

1 Strong fiber
5 River in Germany
8 Indonesian island
12 Alpine comeback
13 Put one's two cents in
14 Midterm, for one
15 Chinese dynasty
16 Different from many
17 Government takeover
18 _____ off me! (stay away or you might get lucky!)
21 Cry of mock horror
22 Moray, e.g.
23 Cheats
26 Imitation gold
30 Long period
31 Represented
32 Red Room equipment
36 Show clearly
39 Before, once
40 Small bird
41 What caused little blip
48 Seaweed gelatin
49 Your of yore
50 Weird
51 Legendary humanoid
52 Dark time for poets
53 Allied to an onion
54 Feel
55 Flirty feature
56 Ice _____

Down

1 Guitar great, Jeff
2 Masseuse's target
3 Manolo, for example
4 Hairpiece
5 Digital tomes
6 Restaurant posting
7 Sound system
8 Become motionless, for lack of wind
9 Nerve-cell part
10 Extol
11 Troublemakers
19 Fine-grained wood
20 All he can think of is _____
23 Wall Street watchdog, abbr.
24 Army rank, abbr.
25 Single-stranded molecules, abbr.
27 Have
28 French lake
29 Purpose
33 Vertigo
34 Sexpert
35 Couch
36 Torch type
37 Fight (for)
38 Thing referred to
41 Faeries
42 S-shaped curve
43 Adjudge
44 He and she
45 Scoundrel
46 Snack choice
47 Youngster

Across

1 Comedian, Sandler
5 Welcome _____
8 Influence
12 Item for sale
13 Reception when he's quietly mad
14 Motorist's route
15 Auditory
16 Relationships with good understanding and trust
18 Dom's look of desire
20 Road-surface material
21 Safari sight
25 Murmur
27 In conflict with, with "of"
31 _____ of luxury
32 Be decisive
33 Started a fire
34 The _____ of the land
35 Baseball's Maglie
36 Perspex weapon of choice
38 Decrepit
39 Letter before iota
41 Orange tuber
43 Control-freak preference
49 Step-up
52 _____-China
53 Rejected proposal
54 _____ start with your performance....
55 Crystal-ball gazer
56 Make a sweater
57 Military rank, abbr.
58 Gouda alternative

Down

1 Illegal desertion, abbr.
2 Information
3 Greek thinker
4 Pilgrimage destination
5 Offensive missile syst., abbr.
6 Palm species
7 Error
8 Walk in mud
9 "This means _____!"
10 Tamandua delight
11 "That's right!"
17 _____ stitch
19 Russell Crowe's middle name
22 Unlucky
23 Do perfectly
24 Opinion piece in a newspaper
25 Outlay
26 Colorful deep-sea fish
28 Winter contagion
29 Lubricate
30 Southwest Indian
36 Derby event
37 One kind of bread
40 Diviner's deck
42 Commence
44 Nonclerical
45 1952 Olympics site
46 Convince
47 What's the big _____?
48 Standard
49 Press
50 Absence of
51 Animation platform, abbr.

Across

1 Conductor, Klemperer
5 School transportation
8 Swerve
12 Knitting method
13 It may follow you
14 That's why
15 Geraint's lady
16 E-mail joking to and fro, for example
18 Surrender to the dom
20 Princess and the _____
21 Deadly fly
25 Ball director
27 Ticket choice
30 Beady-eyed creatures
31 Outdated
32 Playroom item
34 Take off
35 Duty
37 Show a lot of love for
38 "_____ Lady . . .," Bob Dylan
39 New Guinea native
41 17th letter of the Greek alphabet
43 Preferable to e-mail for romantic communications
48 Sea-Tac take-off point
51 It may be bright
52 Needle holder
53 Tax advisor, abbr.
54 Lowest tide
55 "Out of the question"
56 Long period of time
57 Transgresses

Down

1 Oil group, abbr.
2 Sushi fish
3 Detected in a blunder
4 _____ but a goody
5 Hindu for Mr.
6 Caspian feeder
7 Most calm
8 Wood cover
9 Pitcher's performance gauge, abbr.
10 Morning food choice
11 Seafood delicacy
17 "_____ time"
19 Bottom duster
22 Formidable task
23 Walkway, old time
24 See
25 Fence
26 Elbow-wrist connection
28 Military supplies
29 Thick porridge description
33 Native of Belgrade
36 Let him have his way
40 "Thrilla in Manila" participant
42 Poet, Heinrich
44 Mafia chief
45 Hated org. in "Mississippi Burning"
46 Back end
47 Pounds' sounds
48 Detective, abbr.
49 Greek H
50 Vie for office

#37

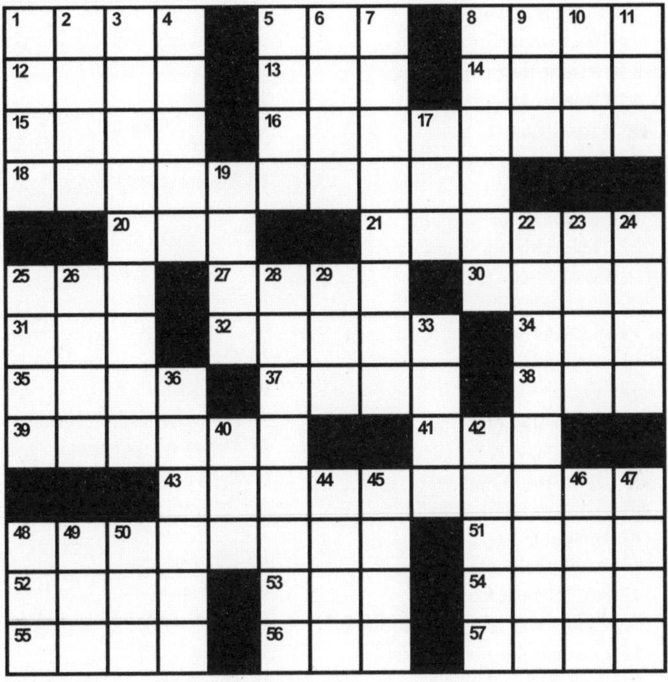

99 Shades of Play

Across

1 Pro's opposite
5 Smidgen
8 Boring triplet
12 Fill
13 Turkish title of rank
14 Ready for picking
15 Cognac for the billionaire
17 Customer
18 Listen, old way
20 Dickens's "A Christmas _____"
23 Be reluctant
26 Stat for Clemens, abbr.
27 Delectable body part when playing pool
30 Quill point
31 Nigerian city
32 Collared
33 Kitchen surface
35 Charged item
36 Cooking utensil
37 Edison contemporary
39 Watched by dieter
42 Feeling great pleasure
45 It will melt on a hot body
49 Anita Baker, for one
50 Child's word for grandmother
51 Obsessively absorbed in him
52 Have on
53 New York time, abbr.
54 Garden of temptation

Down

1 _____ king
2 Neighbor of Swed., abbr.
3 _____-o'-shanter
4 Its license plates say "Famous Potatoes"
5 Comic, Carvey
6 Chinese gelatin
7 Setting
8 Southeast Asian country
9 Fleur-de-_____
10 Emulate
11 1985 Selleck film, "_____ Alibi"
16 Toothpaste type
19 Botches
20 Goes with 50
21 Met expectations
22 Jewish priest
24 Auspices
25 Drivel
27 NBC TV show
28 Idea of oneself
29 Peak near Taormina
31 Bulgarian moola
34 Reader
37 _____-Tac
38 Hair-raising
40 Tapi endings
41 It's overhead
42 Not cooked
43 Inn intake
44 "Harper Valley _____"
46 Pull the plug on
47 Dug in
48 Football night, abbr.

Across

1 Cereal-dish component
4 _____meter
7 Make up one's mind
10 Land outline
12 Sharer's word
13 Jane or John
14 Prepared for kinkiness
17 Part of a conference
18 Modern surgical tool
21 Japanese-American
24 Impersonator
25 They show off clothes
27 Middle of the alphabet letters
28 Ten million rupees
29 Criticize
31 Melody
33 Expression of pride
34 Poker bet
35 Kindness
36 Really good
39 Dom who has lost it description
44 Frequently
45 Expensive vase
46 Slick
47 Furrow maker
48 Schlep
49 "_____ to a Grecian Urn"

Down

1 Photo _____ (camera sessions)
2 "Charlie Tango" reading, abbr.
3 Sticky stuff

4 "My bad"
5 Membership fees
6 Everyday
7 Danish city
8 Luau serving
9 Big Conference number
11 High-voltage gun
15 Part of a price
16 Wavelike design
18 Hasty escape
19 Sleep problem
20 Asian capital
22 Blunder
23 Writer, Asimov
25 Not fair
26 Eternity, almost
28 Material for uniforms
30 Be nosy, like the billionaire snooping on e-mails
32 Missouri feeder
33 Opposite of verso
35 Least amount, abbr.
37 Neutral shade
38 "The _____ and Winding Road," Beatles song
39 Pair with aah
40 Alien flier
41 Formula One Grand Prix site
42 Wizened
43 Strong cleaner

Across

1 Old king in Iran
5 Trailing plant
8 Oscar winner, Paquin
12 Kind of sub
13 Word before "I told you so!"
14 "Crazy" bird
15 Made a touchdown
16 DNA's relative, abbr.
17 Deadly sin
18 Persona of inner goddess when theatened
21 Particular unit
22 It may be white
25 Response to a tickle
29 Indian flatbread
30 Former European grp., abbr.
31 T.G.I.F. part
33 Hoop
35 Unacceptable
38 Tell confidentially
41 Put out
43 _____ Rancho, NM city
44 Subject of a marital spat
49 _____ on the cheek
52 Laters!
53 Stallion's mate
54 Longing
55 Ever, to Keats
56 Independent ruler
57 Match up
58 _____ white wine
59 Prevent

Down

1 Type of carpet
2 Looks hot as _____
3 Song for a diva
4 Long, skinny sandwich
5 Sabra
6 Let off steam
7 Long (for)
8 Word blindness
9 NCO part
10 Gobble month, abbr.
11 "_____ luck?"
19 International bank based in Holland, abbr.
20 Charged bit
23 Wrapped garment
24 Blyton, popular children's writer
25 "_____ Are the Champions"
26 Stopped working, abbr.
27 Fliers' organization, abbr.
28 "Yadda, yadda, yadda," abbr.
32 Black magic
34 Moi?
36 Sand trap
37 Cable network
39 U.S. medical-research branch, abbr.
40 Made bubbles in a bath
42 Put in
45 Ogler
46 Select, in a way
47 Wicked _____
48 Inspiring fear
49 Nipper
50 Horse-and-buggy _____
51 "Avatar" technology, abbr.

Across

1 Returnable envelope, for short
4 Monopolist's portion
7 Arctic, for one
10 Afflict
11 A King Henry
12 Energy
13 Honeymoon dessert
16 Soothing touch
17 Flight part
20 The lady's
23 Hated war, for short
24 Singe
28 Close in on
30 Blood-group system
31 One kind of daddy!
33 Buddy (sl.)
34 Rain cats and dogs
36 Speck of dust
37 Psyche
38 After-lunch sandwich
40 Speck in the ocean
42 Word stressed in the contract
46 Overly studlike
50 Go astray morally
51 Make a serious effort to get something
52 Pledge
53 Conducted
54 Sow's pen
55 Helm heading, abbr.

Down

1 Bursa
2 . . . is the _____ that I breathe . . .
3 Varnish resin
4 Roman welcomes
5 Ad _____
6 Italian money before the Euro
7 Spite
8 Wide-shoe spec
9 One way to go
14 Squashed-grapes leftovers
15 Yuck!
17 Lose it
18 Hard limit, basically
19 French romance
21 Resist the dom!
22 Military rank, abbr.
25 Sing with closed lips
26 Back then
27 Scoundrel
29 Origin
32 Horse controls
35 Log
39 Sound of delight
41 Hot spot
43 Bags
44 Agitation
45 Whirl
46 Rolodex abbreviation
47 Neighbor of Ida., abbr.
48 Back-to-work day, abbr.
49 Farm female

Across

1 Wild guess
5 Rocky pinnacle
8 Cotton bundle
12 Sly trick
13 "_____ you kidding?"
14 March 15
15 Elementary particle
16 Stop color
17 Lincoln penny
18 Escaped from the grip of the dom?
21 Letters before an alias
22 "_____ Gang"
23 Bummer
26 Small three-masted vessels
30 Together
31 CEO training step, abbr.
32 Old-mansion decoration
36 Unlikely to qualify as a sub
39 Keats piece
40 Intend
41 Even the arteries feel it
47 That's so _____!
48 Stop biting it!
49 Field of study
50 Push
51 Complied with the dom
52 Farm soil
53 "When I _____ You," Leo Sayer tune
54 Scratch the surface of
55 Poker stake

Down

1 Spoils
2 Jackson 5 member
3 Gazillions
4 Whine
5 Kind of sauce
6 Cookie
7 Sly creature
8 Antacid, abbr.
9 Red Sea city
10 Loan
11 Dover time, abbr.
19 Hawaiian guitar, abbr.
20 Appearance
23 Vet
24 Kim ending
25 It's catching
27 Printers' widths
28 Media company
29 Articulate
33 Forested
34 Nigerian
35 Madhouse
36 Billionaire opposite
37 Developer of Blackberry
38 African antelope
41 Yawn maker
42 Balcony section
43 Type of bread
44 "Pumping _____"
45 Uncluttered
46 Up for it
47 She had one to handle the ransom demander

Across

1 Dances noisily
5 Punishment tool
8 It has strings attached
12 Surface space
13 Tankard filler
14 Gift from billionaire
15 Spanking body part
16 Coriander
18 Get mad with a T-shirt?
20 Damage
21 "Savvy?"
22 Game plan
26 Holy man
30 Frying liquid
31 Makes a contented sound
33 Trim branches
34 Nasty
36 Military chaplain
38 Chew and swallow
40 Packed away
41 Chef all worked up?
46 Cattle breed
47 Opera-house box
49 Sunrise point
50 Health _____
51 Eye color
52 Victim
53 Tit for _____
54 Sac

Down

1 Pick
2 Kuwaiti, for example
3 Helter-skelter
4 Polynesian
5 Suggestive
6 Mélange
7 Deceptive
8 Door-frame part
9 _____ the challenge; able to do something
10 Diamond cover
11 Period in Japanese history
17 Make, in arithmetic
19 Put a blanket around, with up
22 Old French coin
23 Nicotine fix
24 Most out of practice
25 Nettle
27 Story with a message
28 Low
29 Clever
32 Argue over dom's orders, e.g.
35 Zesty
37 Leaning to the right
39 Mural
41 Skyrocket
42 Alternate
43 Mangrove palm
44 Mosquito
45 Athena's shield
46 Savvy
48 Albany clock setting, abbr.

#43

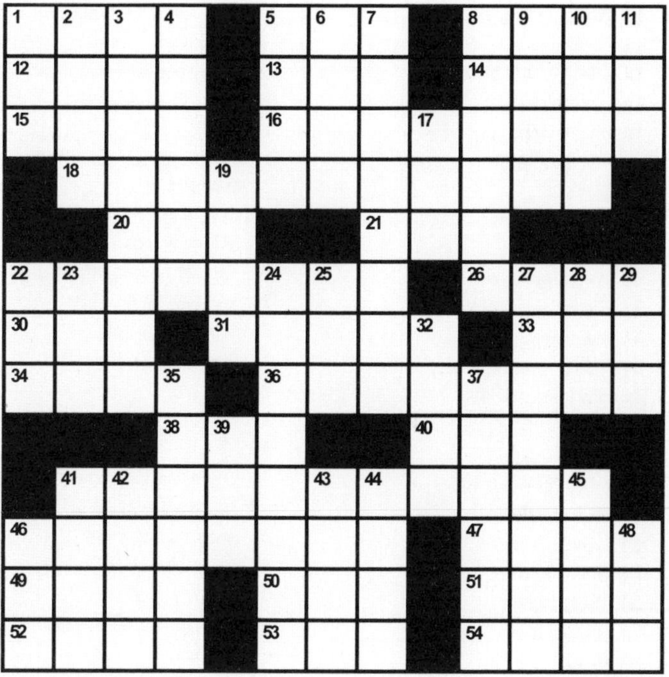

99 Shades of Play

Across

1 Denver height
5 _____ about him
8 Neighbor of Cambodia
12 State
13 Attorneys' org., abbr.
14 Facts
15 Open-court hearing
16 Colt maker
18 Shake up
20 Sudden burst
23 Dark
27 Boat with a well-used bed
31 Miss. neighbor, abbr.
32 It's found in banks
33 Push for payment
34 Ink mover
35 Land of opportunity, abbr.
36 Black vehicle attached to a bracelet
39 Beat
41 Run-down
42 Submissives united!
46 At a regular pace
49 Open
53 Make well
54 Wine cask
55 Intertwine
56 Ruin
57 Gender
58 Go along with

Down

1 Infamous Chinese politico
2 Climbing plant
3 Filmmaker, Spike
4 List of errors
5 Wise three
6 Adjoin
7 _____ Point, CA
8 Smallest detectable sensation
9 Blackbird
10 Many times
11 Musical-scale note
17 Wow
19 Dark-blue sapphire, for example
20 Recruiter
21 Mince words
22 Special Forces unit
24 Weapon of knights
25 Trojan War epic
26 Brindled
28 Big fuss
29 Go (of a car)
30 "Then what?"
36 Over-noisy or colorful
37 The Buckeyes, abbr.
38 Astronomer's sighting
40 Sacred song
43 Bridle parts
44 The Detroit connection was one
45 Wildcat
46 "Pipe down!"
47 Earl Grey, for one
48 Something to nibble on
50 San Francisco hill
51 Anonymous John
52 Decide to leave, with "out"

Across

1 Salami server
5 Anaconda kin
8 Gaucho's weapon
12 Kind of column
13 Orchid arrangements
14 Wishes undone
15 Quote
16 Fruit-tree collections
18 Chivalric smooch
20 Carolina
21 "_____ all in a day's work"
22 Stain
24 Black, abbr.
27 Burglar
31 Easter item
32 Chase vehicle
34 Formally known as
35 "Naked Maja" painter
37 Level top of a mountain
38 Do a background check like the billionaire, for example
39 Society newcomer, abbr.
41 "So _____ me!"
43 Red Room key name
47 Doubters
49 Community
51 "Body _____," Kathleen Turner movie
52 A sentence starter
53 Olympic fencing weapon
54 Wet behind the _____
55 Pilot's announcement, briefly
56 Kick back

Down

1 Medic
2 Large-scale
3 Laziness
4 Philosophies
5 "Thanks _____!"
6 Dehydrated
7 What is harvested
8 Harsh and metallic
9 Yours, mine, and _____
10 Certain digital watch face, abbr.
11 Idiot
17 Deliver punishment
19 Gardening tools locale
22 _____abyte
23 In times past
25 WWII crater
26 Horatian work
28 Wrapper
29 Turn
30 Acquire
33 Big _____ Conference
36 Pros
40 DC time setting, abbr.
42 Absolute
43 Vintage designation
44 Genuine
45 On the Atlantic
46 Wool sources
47 The car, affectionately
48 New Zealand parrot
50 Cyberspace

99 Shades of Play

Across

1 Boat trailer
5 Back-to-work time, abbr.
8 Bricklaying equipment
12 Monitor brand
13 Greek letter
14 Back door
15 Monk
16 Upholstery problem
17 Impose, as a tax
18 Rouge boundary not to be crossed
21 Dom's constant insistence
22 Promise of a payback, abbr.
23 Playroom scent
26 She has to have it all the time
30 It makes one hot
31 Big bird of stories
32 Beef stick, for example
36 Arrival
39 Kook
40 Go after, in a way
41 Disapproved color for the Saab
47 Shut the door harshly
48 Trouble
49 What they eventually fell into
50 Hoop type
51 Microprocessor chip, abbr.
52 Patron
53 Manolo part
54 Ability to hit a target
55 Insignificant

Down

1 Street or flower
2 S.A. palm
3 Dole's running mate, 1996
4 Desk item
5 Is worthy of
6 Symbi followers
7 Table-setting piece
8 Balloon filler
9 Strong team
10 Nightclub
11 Pork place
19 Greek cross
20 Actress, Myrna
23 1991 alliance, abbr.
24 Kind of contribution, abbr.
25 Rolodex no., abbr.
27 There was never a _____nup
28 Darling
29 Scorpio-sign month, abbr.
33 Kind of instinct
34 Coffee holder
35 NY college town
36 Refugee's request
37 Expected
38 Cream-colored paper
41 Code _____, billionaire security phrase
42 Congested-lung sound
43 Indian lodging (var.)
44 Always afraid to _____ him
45 Through
46 Lived
47 "Zip it!"

Across

1 It was _____ at first sight!
5 Relaxed, in a way
8 Like a desert
12 Small case
13 Strange object in the sky, abbr.
14 One way to run
15 Coming-out girls, abbr.
16 Rage
17 Adjust a piano
18 Kind of routine
21 Yours, old way
23 "That's a _____!"
26 Mom's hours of labor
30 Animal house
32 Clay, formerly
33 French sculptor, Jean
34 Andy Warhol painting
35 "Maggie May" singer, Stewart
36 Outbursts of nastiness
39 Mariners, for example
41 Pretentious
42 Blockbuster
46 Verb with thou
49 Rural sight
50 Not yet final
53 What an unrequited heart might do
54 Billionaire's wife title
55 Bug
56 Shout derisively at
57 Drain of strength
58 Bacon and _____

Down

1 Started the beating
2 Type of truck
3 Split into smaller sections
4 Herb-flavored tea
5 Billionaire office wear
6 '60s do
7 Three-_____ sloth
8 Nymph chaser
9 Like a penguin, in a way
10 Hollywood director, first name
11 Live on the edge of existence
19 Tokyo token
20 Grass part
21 Russian ruler
22 Serf
24 Confessing
25 Bogs and mosses
27 Chi preceder
28 Hesitant sounds
29 Old vinyl records, abbr.
31 Meddlesome
36 Thinking sound . . .
37 Exclamation of impatience
38 Border of hair
40 September bloom
43 Donations
44 Some transfusions
45 Door latch
46 Islam's global gathering
47 Top race-car driver
48 "_____ Loves You," 1964 hit
51 Hang
52 _____ a good plan!

99 Shades of Play

Across

1 On the peak of
5 Boys
8 Struggle for air
12 Crumbly soil
13 Beast of burden
14 Skunk's defense
15 Printing term
16 Bright-colored flower
18 Subject of a $24,000 auction bid
20 Howdy!
21 Vampirelike fly
24 Sot's sound, for short
27 Finish a drive
30 "Gangs of New York" conflict
31 Dark beer
32 Dom's smile, often
34 Johnson or Morrison
35 Brook
37 Despicable
38 Neocene, for one
39 African republic
41 Transcendental number
43 Not listening to the dom, for example
47 A favorite song from Dionne Warwick
49 Trick
52 Kind of exam
53 Double-cross
54 Romantic couple
55 Uncanny
56 Needle point
57 Genesis brother

Down

1 Sound booster
2 Indo-Chinese language
3 Boat in "Jaws"
4 Spatter
5 Exaggerated PR
6 Make
7 Scampers
8 More bloody
9 Angelina Jolie, _____ parent
10 Call for help, abbr.
11 Before
17 Lady
19 Blips
22 Take wing
23 Lab burner
24 Do damage to
25 Bones
26 Mobile phone
28 Atmosphere
29 Routing word
33 French military cap
36 In a long and lean manner
40 "Charlie Tango" investigation question
42 Film type
44 Coal color
45 Fraction of a newton
46 Grit
47 Tribulation
48 "Chances _____"
50 Stew ingredient
51 Bird that doesn't't fly

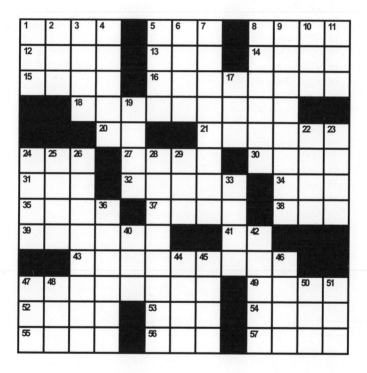

99 Shades of Play

Across

1 Time past
5 Home of "Law and Order"
8 Econ. yardstick, abbr.
11 Actor, Wilson
12 In the style of
13 Be laid up
14 Just how angry can a dom get?
17 Be of use to
18 Strategic advantages
22 Patch up
24 Civil-disorder participant
27 Duty
30 Store, as corn
31 The dom wants her flexible, like this
32 Cuttlefish ejections
33 Salt or pepper
37 Violin, for short
38 Subconscious's clothing, sometimes
45 "The Way I _____," from Timbaland
46 Corleone, for one
47 Triathlete, with man
48 Fraternity members
49 Photo _____ (media events)
50 Salamander

8 Chatter
9 Goose egg
10 Work at
15 Bathroom in London
16 Gum used as a thickener
18 Northern Scandinavians
19 Run off
20 Acid dye
21 Smart
22 Towel word
23 Cassowary relation
25 Large northern deer
26 Legal matters
28 Destroy the tires
29 Roman shield formation
34 Lowest deck of a warship
35 Tandoori sides
36 Ego's pals
38 Broadside
39 'Fore
40 Scout group
41 Siblings
42 Embitterment
43 Column's counterpart
44 Nitroglycerin, abbr.

Down

1 "Yeah, _____!"
2 Have a pink slip for it
3 Southern soldier, abbr.
4 Dallas to NY, abbr.
5 Innocent, when met the billionaire
6 To dim
7 Beluga egg

49

Across

1 Found in a university
5 Stylish
8 Cafeteria carrier
12 Campus site
13 Bed-in enthusiast
14 Ballyhoo
15 Offer to do something naughty (goes with 44 across)
17 Take home
18 Baby-care area
20 Way too weighty
23 DEA investigator
26 Feel the _____
27 Honeymoon marks
29 Asphalt
30 Flood-preventing embankment
31 Subway alternative
33 Spanish gentlemen
35 Maori dance
36 Ancient marker
37 Closet material
38 Railroad car with a bar
41 Act in collusion
44 See 15 across
48 Body of an organism
49 Quaker cereal
50 Not one _____
51 60 minutes
52 Formerly
53 Paralyzed

Down

1 _____ Beta Kappa
2 Controlled
3 Worn
4 Strip a whale
5 Field worker
6 Travel lodges
7 Macho male states
8 _____ beautiful to watch!
9 Knotted weave
10 Yearly interest rate, abbr.
11 Hankering
16 Suggestive stick
19 Don Juan
20 Loophole
21 Impudence
22 "Snowy" bird
24 Tropical gymnosperm
25 Honshu city
27 From this point on
28 _____ got a secret
30 Take it easy
32 Setting of many jokes
34 Bee food
35 Destructive drug
37 Spending limit
39 Highlands hillside
40 Sheep shelter
41 Furniture wood
42 Crowd disapproval
43 Kiwi comparable
45 A pittance
46 Teller alternative, abbr.
47 Chem classroom

50

Across

1 Caps
5 Attorney's thing
8 Honey drink
12 Ruler
13 To the point
14 Scandinavian port
15 Keepsake
17 ID item
18 Silly smile of triumph (goes with 49 across)
20 Twilled cotton
22 Detective (sl.)
23 Make calls
24 Indian bean
28 The first matter, according to scientists
30 Be obligated
31 Long stretches
33 Succeed and thrive
35 Stock advice
36 Milk variety
37 Hard to satisfy
39 Attracting, with a lip bite, perhaps
43 Teacher
44 British statesman
47 They, in Trieste
48 Roth, maybe, abbr.
49 See 18 across
50 Beowulf, for one
51 Crag
52 Garden with a snake

Down

1 Outmoded, with been
2 Signifying a time in the past
3 Religious acolyte
4 Dwarf juniper
5 Indian queen
6 Cast-of-thousands film
7 Peacock, for example
8 Lens for correcting defective vision in one eye
9 Famous twin
10 Charity money
11 The buck stops here
16 "Shogun's" capital
19 Green area
20 Shout
21 1965 Beatles movie
24 Correct text
25 Wonderment
26 Shard of pottery
27 Spanish liqueur
29 Religious buildings
32 007, for one
34 Small coin
37 Pine tree
38 Grammar topic
39 Cutting edge
40 Estimate follower
41 Amateur
42 Nicholas was the last one
43 It precedes aitch
45 Recline
46 Hostel

51

Across

1 Demonstrate
5 Christmas worker
8 Cash cache
12 Certain something
13 New beginning
14 Conception
15 Song for the family (goes with 41 and 33 across)
17 _____room
18 Demure
19 Fold
21 Reject her affection
24 Lyric poem
25 Debauchery
26 For the time being
29 Ward heeler
30 Ashes holder
31 Japanese money
33 See 15 across
36 Smooth
37 Assent
38 Pocohontas, for one
39 Attack on "Charlie Tango"
41 See 15 across
42 Type of cuisine
43 Labyrinth builder in Greek mythology
48 Saxophone
49 Whole
50 Brit's "Baloney!"
51 Mirrors of the soul
52 Little nibble
53 Rapier

Down

1 Adage
2 "What's that?"
3 Metal mixture
4 Watchword
5 Deadly sin
6 Stan who created Spider-Man
7 Without hope
8 Fur cape
9 Just lying around
10 Faithful and true to a Glaswegian
11 Position horizontally
16 Seemingly forever
20 Turmoil
21 Bribe
22 Ship's front
23 Jamaican fruit
26 All for it
27 Biblical birthright seller
28 Smaller plateau
30 Kampala inhabitant
32 Unprecedented
34 Antibodies
35 Famous lion
36 Regard as same
38 Landscape grass
39 Yawl call
40 Recherche
41 Canine cry
42 Everyday article
44 Aka Cassius Clay
45 Chop off
46 Occupy
47 That female

#52

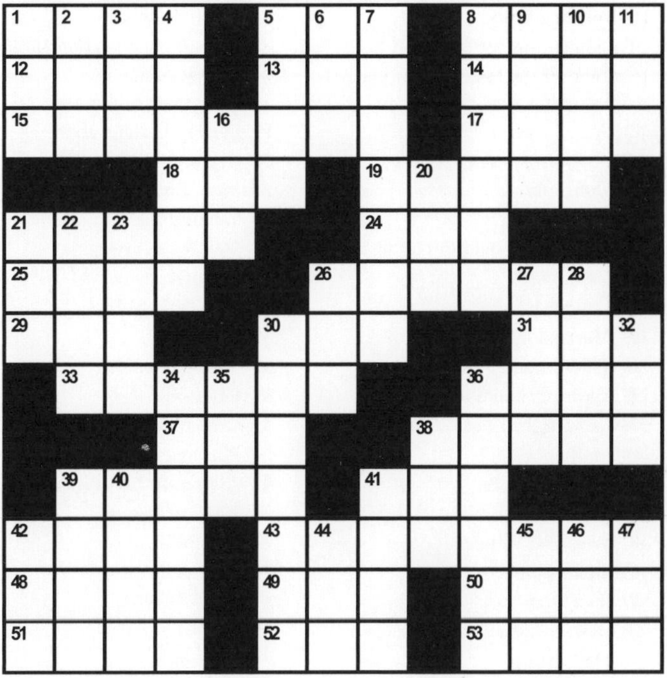

99 Shades of Play

Across

1 Cutting edge
5 Costume mo., abbr.
8 Ear related
12 A way to start
13 Jimmy a door
14 Striped Christmas candy
15 Pastrami purveyor
16 Listening device
17 Spoon measurement, abbr.
18 Food preference, after little blip
21 Continue
22 Well-known
24 Large-mammal hunter
27 Delicious
28 Long fish
29 Married John
31 Tibet's capital
35 Dashing, like the billionaire
38 Lady of the house
39 Malicious
40 The billionaire
45 Raised stand
47 Well-known beer
48 Small salmon
49 It's a wrap!
50 Bass, for one
51 Hate group
52 Not following orders fallout
53 Shade maker
54 Yin's opposite

3 Wall Street order
4 Original and first
5 First act
6 Ocean entree
7 Dom, at his worst
8 Groups of eight
9 Billiard felt area, for example
10 Sitting pols
11 Delectable mushroom
19 Portland's state, abbr.
20 Region of India
23 Metric unit of force
24 You and me
25 Spot for steering the cat
26 Spanish palace
30 French for gold
32 Nimble
33 "Gunsmoke" bartender
34 Pond cells
35 Crown for royalty
36 Pharmacists' white
37 Taking the 5 mil was a _____
move
41 Kittiwake
42 RC, e.g.
43 Asian ruler
44 Carol
45 Blockhead
46 Travel need

Down

1 North Atlantic fishes
2 Eye section

53

Across

1 Cricket club
4 Word on all U.S. coins
7 It takes _____ to tango!
10 Taj Mahal city
12 Arrogance
13 Make one
14 Ukraine city
15 Recently produced for the first time
16 "Do _____ others as . . ."
17 Free to move around the bed
20 French street
21 Bakery supply
24 Put down on paper
28 Cuff connector
30 One billion years or so
31 Backtalk
33 _____ Tolstoy
34 Add
37 Cannes painting subject
40 The "back"
42 Kind of deer
43 The older, other woman
48 Hemingway nickname
51 Snake pet
52 Idea
53 Merit
54 Electric-guitar hookup
55 Lift
56 Reporter's question
57 "Indubitably"
58 The Who song "Love, Reign _____ Me"

Down

1 Capital on the Caspian
2 Fer or _____ it!
3 Not kosher
4 Refined
5 S-shaped molding
6 Gift from will
7 Huge amount
8 Intelligence
9 Julian's mother
11 Forestall
13 Son of Jacob
18 Pyramid king
19 Post-WWII trade group, for short
22 Exchange for money
23 Echelon
24 Nurse type
25 Cross
26 Enjoying
27 "_____/Tuck"
29 Vetoes
32 Possibly
35 City related
36 Tire meas., abbr.
38 Money to be gained
39 Parrot landing
41 Held off
44 Draw near
45 Mix
46 Gospel writer
47 Lascivious look
48 Sunday seat
49 Sound of a good massage
50 Veteran

Across

1 End of a Spanish greeting
5 Fit to be dragged
8 Red-skinned cheese
12 Hawkeye state
13 There's much about nothing
14 Zoo enclosure
15 Get annoyed at the bed
18 Copy
19 By-product of winemaking
22 Body of good conduct
26 Loungers
30 Fountain order
31 Johnson work
32 Architectural projection
34 Mork's gal, abbr.
35 Champagne color, often
37 Revolution
39 Ringworm
41 Sorority letter
42 Persian silk
46 Use flirting weapons
52 Dark doings
53 Aromatic drink
54 Plan that could be naughty and nice!
55 Characteristic carrier
56 Hardy animal
57 Tip-top

Down

1 Party bowlful
2 Marker, abbr.
3 Barley beard
4 Relating to some vertebrae
5 Living-room light source
6 Pastoral poem
7 Indian helmet
8 Conspicuous successes
9 East Indian sauce
10 Past
11 Kitten's cry
16 Prefix with centric
17 Word with box or pick
19 Take on
20 Arm bones
21 Astronaut, John
23 Hip-hop "bro"
24 Fool
25 Showy flowered plant
27 Drop the ball
28 Brazilian "grand prix" town
29 Match part
33 Serving from the secretary
36 Corn type
38 Sister of Calliope
40 Word to a doctor
43 Greek-salad cheese
44 Service charges
45 Falcon nestling
46 _____ to differ
47 Map abbreviation
48 Cake pan
49 Wedding answer
50 Retreat
51 Envelope that comes back to you, abbr.

1	2	3	4		5	6	7		8	9	10	11
12					13				14			
15				16				17				
			18									
19	20	21						22		23	24	25
26					27	28	29		30			
31				32				33		34		
35			36		37				38			
39				40				41				
			42		43	44	45					
46	47	48								49	50	51
52					53				54			
55					56				57			

99 Shades of Play

Across

1 Robert the Bruce, e.g.
5 "60 Minutes" network
8 Bankrolls
12 Colorful deep-sea fish
13 Retirement fund, abbr.
14 "Star Trek" character
15 Rani's wear
16 Happy, like a schoolgirl
18 Perfume ingredient
20 Relationship milestone
23 A rechargeable battery
27 A.S., for example
31 Performances for one
32 The love _____
33 Ladder rung
35 Free (of)
36 Ms. Brockovich
38 Preferred tea
40 Made over
42 Brag
43 Place name
47 Sauvignon blanc was a favorite one
50 Capital of Azerbaijan
54 Roman numeral on a watch dial
55 "_____ the Season"
56 Tennessee's state flower
57 Prohibition
58 Take steps
59 Formally surrender

Down

1 Funk band
2 Tax prep. expert, abbr.
3 Crew member
4 Appetite
5 Butts
6 Camembert's cousin
7 Edible starch
8 "Die Hard" actor
9 "When We Were Kings" subject
10 Cacophony
11 Lose oomph
17 Pink-lady ingredient
19 Inventor, Elisha
20 _____ optic cable
21 Condition
22 Inflexible like the dom
24 Bony part that resembles a horn
25 Straighten
26 Biblical verb
28 Liable
29 Fan setting
30 Travel on the mountains
34 Maliciousness
37 Dummy
39 Pentameter type
41 "Stupid me!"
44 Kind of bread
45 Auricular
46 Place that allows "eggs-tradition"
47 Movie format, abbr.
48 Brazilian hot spot
49 Dark and feminine (Chinese)
51 "We _____ the World"
52 Tease
53 "It's no _____!"

56

Across

1 Respectful address
5 Computer part, abbr.
8 Guru
12 "Not to mention . . ."
13 It may be tipped
14 Agreement word
15 Section in the newspaper, abbr.
16 Miss _____
17 Prying
18 Seismic climax effects
21 Personal
22 Exist
23 Protections
26 Rub the wrong way
30 Snake in the grass
31 Voice
32 Show off your _____
36 Billionaire hair color
39 Greensward
40 Saddler's tool
41 Ransom demand
46 Hindu clothing
47 Eastern sash
48 Fifty-fifty
50 Car-rental agency
51 Order to attack, with "on"
52 Excellent
53 Entanglement
54 Bother
55 Whole bunch

Down

1 _____ jacket
2 Love song
3 "_____ I care!"
4 Slogans
5 Gets agitated
6 What the realtor made to the billionaire
7 Salt Lake City inhabitant
8 Surgical knife
9 Out of control
10 Confusion
11 No matter what
19 Ram's mate
20 Exploration target
23 Time in history
24 76 product
25 _____ all over
27 Rap on a window
28 Deception
29 Do wrong
33 Mischievous
34 Billionaire's shirt
35 Fried turnover
36 Cotton fabric
37 Night bird
38 Toolbox item
41 Cell phone entry
42 Flower
43 Citing word
44 Track
45 "Scream" star, Campbell
46 Everybody's Uncle
49 Without precedent

Across

1 "By yesterday," abbr.
5 "Told ya!"
8 Racing vehicle
12 Equitable
13 Seeds
14 Computer image
15 Beginner
16 Sorry for getting mad
18 Crazies
20 Bawl out
23 Southwestern shrubs
27 NHL great
28 Mosque leader
31 Changed the direction
32 Small amount
33 Like some pools
35 Led
36 Ended
38 Bad idea
39 Lend a hand
40 One of the Gorgons in Greek mythology
42 Ankle-bracelet attachments
44 Marks the margins
47 Guy who sleeps with everyone
50 Music genre
54 Province
55 Net holder
56 Farm unit
57 Slightly wet
58 Squawk
59 Big jerk

Down

1 Toward the stern
2 Put into words
3 _____ ball (bad shot in basketball)
4 Move around like a predator
5 Kachina doll makers
6 Say for sure
7 Jack-of-all-trades
8 Pretentious bad taste
9 Flawless serve
10 Harry Potter's best friend
11 Demolition stuff, abbr.
17 Informal acknowledgment of debt, abbr.
19 Revise
20 Biblical city
21 Desire eagerly
22 Spherical
24 Pink color
25 Efficacy
26 Propels
29 Menacing
30 Bother
34 Stud site
37 Where models strut
41 Fifth note in a musical scale
43 Dissertation
45 Solo
46 Part-time worker, perhaps
47 Like some scientists
48 "_____ you kidding?"
49 NYC part
51 S. American tuber
52 Cremation vase
53 Animal show-off spot

58

99 Shades of Play

Across

1 Do nothing
5 Parking place
8 _____ good example
12 Northern Japanese people
13 Mrs. John Lennon
14 Playroom tool
15 Divine
17 Ecstatic in a blanket
18 Seedless orange
20 Synthetic resin
23 Numbered composition
26 Lady's man
27 The spice of life!
30 Place for a pedi
31 OK, in a way
32 Before, to Coleridge
34 The billionaire became one, ideal guy
36 Copacabana site
37 Big Bang matter
38 Bird related
40 An artist of consummate skill
44 Food thickener
47 Bracelet metal
51 Stuffed chicken
52 Tiny particle
53 One teaspoon, maybe
54 Saunter
55 "The Amazing Race" network
56 Whack

Down

1 Chem classroom
2 Lamp liquid
3 Game-show request
4 Detail oriented
5 Certain apartment
6 Burden of proof
7 Cough-syrup ingredient
8 Row
9 Notable time
10 Leading
11 Likely
16 Regrettable
19 Work hard
20 Mule
21 Cheeky
22 African enclosure
24 Reproductive organs
25 Mideast land
27 Do nothing (sl.)
28 Of yore
29 Fled, after the overzealous dom scene
31 Tibetan monk
33 Ages and ages
35 Eliminate
38 Oils and such
39 Annuls
41 "Ben Hur," e.g.
42 Untidy one
43 Browns on a Cannes beach
44 Take a downhill ride
45 Tutor
46 Gooey stuff
48 This moment
49 "_____ Today"
50 Ran into

1	2	3	4		5	6	7		8	9	10	11
12					13				14			
15				16					17			
		18						19				
20	21	22						23		24	25	
26					27	28	29					
30				31						32		33
	34		35							36		
	37							38	39			
		40		41	42	43						
44	45	46			47					48	49	50
51					52				53			
54					55				56			

Across

1 Santa's helper
4 Galley tool
7 Packed out
11 Rustic locale
12 One in a suit
13 Nabisco cookie
14 They do it at 35,000 feet
17 Certain apartments
18 A farewell remark
21 Laid-back
25 Really bad coffee
26 Archipelago member
29 Alleviate
30 Stretch
31 Ice-sculptured birds
33 Use knots
34 Radiant look
36 Turned on by
37 "We need to get a cat!"
38 Positively state one's position
40 Aaron and Raymond
42 Domains ruled by a Duke
45 Strip slowly
50 Make eyes at
51 It needs refinement
52 SUV, abbr.
53 Slow
54 Repeated refusals to the boss's advances
55 Burmese coin

Down

1 Spreading tree
2 Muumuu go-with
3 Two-faced
4 Diamond Head locale
5 Bitter
6 Military unit
7 Ship section
8 Internet letters
9 Romanian-mint product
10 Court ploy
15 Needle cases
16 Ground breaker
18 One-celled organism
19 Ellington and Wellington
20 Philosophies
22 Subsequently
23 Willow tree
24 Quite a while
27 Turn on
28 Office-computer link, abbr.
32 Judicious
35 Jumbled assortment
39 Grind
41 Consume entirely
43 Medal recipient
44 Dangerous time
45 Soda
46 Dom's problem
47 Antlered animal
48 Hog's home
49 Mermaid's home

60

99 Shades of Play

Across
1 Right away, abbr.
5 _____cup (odd sound)
8 Physics particle
12 He had _____bucks
13 Egg cells
14 Bainbridge is one
15 First part of a radio comedy
16 A herd of whales
17 Put on board, as cargo
18 "Going north" easily or dictatorial?
21 Ring count
22 Tennis great, Chris
25 Can't stand
28 Regenerated
29 19th Greek letter
30 Popular sushi fish
32 Passion
36 Convents
39 It may be fixed
40 Carefree
41 Post-breakfast hygiene
46 Desensitize
49 It loves to hug
50 Vigor
51 Certainly not tongue-tied
52 Inch one-sixths
53 Barks
54 Plum variety
55 After expenses
56 Latin infinitive

Down
1 Female servant

2 Before circle and final
3 Worked up
4 Iranian language
5 Navajo structures
6 Nobelist, Pavlov
7 Walt Whitman's hometown
8 Plant fungi
9 Canada's neighbor, abbr.
10 Past
11 Born (Fr.)
19 _____ Royal Highness
20 Time of anticipation
23 Mesh of veins
24 Cafeteria carrier
25 _____ ease
26 Pastoral sounds
27 Distress
31 Computer department, for short
33 Play around
34 John Boyd _____, nutritionist and Nobel Prize winner
35 Deli order
36 Horrified
37 _____ an eyelid
38 A farewell remark
42 A smattering of
43 Days
44 Peaks
45 Douse
46 Vetoes
47 Dot-com's address, abbr.
48 Cultural Revolution leader

61

Across

1 Airport times, abbr.
5 Subs have to stay _____
8 Evening-news producers
11 Brazen
12 Detergent brand
13 Turn on a pivot
14 76 station
15 Best, of picks, for example
16 Remedy
17 Won't leave the ladies alone
20 Knock off
21 Gasteyer of "Saturday Night Live"
22 London WC
24 Contract adjustment
30 Turkish title of rank
31 Pendulum's path
32 Society-page word
33 Champagne fave
37 Syndicate head
38 Jackanape
39 In-vitro items
41 Too control freaky
46 Ponder
47 "Happy Jack" singers
48 Thickener
50 Jury member
51 One billion years
52 Granular snow
53 24 a day, abbr.
54 _____ de Montmartre
55 Liquid remnant

Down

1 Antipollution org., abbr.
2 Maryland athlete, for short
3 Relating to docs in storage
4 Person who endures hardship
5 Greek cheese
6 Like a dom's will
7 Gene Kelly's forte
8 Hint
9 Prickle
10 Realize
13 Split
18 Untilled tract
19 Wind up
22 Experiment room
23 Days past
25 Workers available
26 Unit of force
27 Imperil
28 Modern, prefix
29 Bo Derek rating
34 Prisoner
35 Global financiers, abbr.
36 Degenerate
40 Delicious dish
41 Court petitioner
42 Exploits
43 Cream puff
44 Steak sauce
45 Crumpled
46 How fast, abbr.
49 Coffee order, abbr.

62

Across

1 Unit of electrical resistance
4 Like some receptions
7 For every
10 Polynesian paste
11 Tower
13 Leave dumbstruck
14 Leaves a smooch all the way down
17 Highbrow
18 Brave person
19 Jocularity
21 No-man's-land
24 Death pretender
28 Asian breads
30 Tighten when needed
31 Atmospheric content
33 Tax that led to a party in Boston
34 Architectural projection
37 Crush
40 Acid/alcohol compound
42 "_____ Send Me"
43 Ancient
45 Tie up loose _____
48 Madly in love
52 _____ Wednesday
53 Craving
54 "_____ to Joy"
55 No way
56 Golf-bag item
57 So untrue!

Down

1 Exercises choice
2 Unicorn feature
3 Cat cries
4 Not so good
5 Truncheon
6 Country bumpkin
7 Faux _____ (mistake)
8 Fleece provider
9 Matter for a judge
12 Cooking wine
15 Old World bird
16 Organism body
20 Jerk
22 Soak leather
23 Valet tips
24 Hawaiian fish
25 Like a virgin
26 Elevator man
27 Warhol subject
29 Airline to Stockholm
32 Gather intelligence
35 Arrival times, for short
36 Permitted
38 T. S. Eliot or Robert Frost
39 Humorous U.S. writer
41 Come back on
44 Two tablets, maybe
46 Birdbrain
47 Hard fat
48 One of the Bobbsey twins
49 July 4th celebrant
50 Possessive thou
51 Colorado Native Americans

63

Across

1 Get inside data
4 Hangout
7 Luau serving
10 Pirate's "yes"
11 Slice of history
12 Toys, with sex
13 Mesmerized
16 Before (poet.)
17 Turn away
18 Tumult
22 Minable metal
23 "Seinfeld" character
24 Rounded hills
28 Doofus
29 In _____ of (instead)
30 Five Nations tribe
33 One way to run
35 Its symbol is an omega
36 Keep trying to tie her down
37 Coral Sea inlet
40 Moray, e.g.
41 Obsession
46 Logan postings, abbr.
47 Seaman's reference
48 Pile of rocks
49 Ran into
50 Musical scale note
51 Nelly Furtado song

Down

1 SW Missouri river
2 Burmese coin
3 Affirmative statement
4 "Heavens to Betsy!"
5 Gaelic language
6 Drop off
7 Stack up
8 Stink
9 Ain't correct?
12 Jaw related
14 Stripling
15 Take in
18 Not for ladies
19 Sheltered, nautically
20 Tale
21 Secret places
22 Approve
25 Old Italian bread
26 Elder and Majors
27 Foam
31 Blacken
32 Morning time, abbr.
33 Mideast money
34 _____ before the storm
37 Rhythmical lines
38 Chamber starter
39 Marshy material
40 Reiterate
42 Lunkhead
43 Computer training center, abbr.
44 _____'wester
45 Like some wines

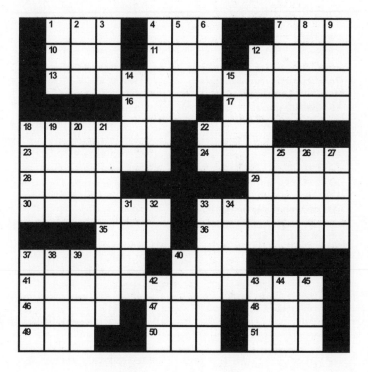

64

99 Shades of Play

Across

1 Door part
5 Elite group
8 Cool guy
12 In excess of
13 Rink surface
14 Metal
15 Below alpha
16 Chains of love?
18 Managed to make him uptight
20 Oft-mentioned 19th-century romantic wriiter
23 Breads
27 Diminishable
31 Nut
32 Silent assent
33 How she avoided the harassing editor
35 Sub must do this to stay in good condition
36 Weight
38 Reckless boldness
40 Dom's aid
42 Ink
43 Point at
47 Is this type of beauty just too radiant?
50 Mountain lion
54 Aviation agency, abbr.
55 Tell it like it isn't
56 Glimpse
57 Brings spirit
58 Unpaired
59 Dom's reaction to disobedience

Down

1 Position
2 Penn. is one, abbr.
3 Got introduced
4 West German politician
5 Closed hand
6 Authentic
7 Whip mark
8 African antelope
9 WWW address, abbr.
10 Fawn's mother
11 Naval rank, abbr.
17 Mushroom you can eat
19 Nestling hawks
20 Suspends
21 End a mission, for example
22 Detection technology
24 Wheels setting
25 Winged
26 Half-human, half-horse deity
28 Diner sandwich, abbr.
29 Caustic solution
30 Glade shade
34 Himalayan mystery
37 Passover breads
39 Kind of room
41 Crony
44 Metric weight
45 "Idylls of the King" lady
46 Long in the tooth
47 Swim
48 Poker high card
49 Stun
51 Dos Passos trilogy
52 Automobile sticker fig., abbr.
53 Word of support

65

Across

1 Leg section
5 Cell phone, smart card, abbr.
8 Gear
11 Small quantity
12 Win the heart of
13 Mr. Gershwin
14 Sailing reminder of the playroom
17 Virgo mo., abbr.
18 Safari sight
19 Refine, as metal
22 Palace dweller
25 Curse
26 Provocatively shy
27 Show
28 With sorrow
30 Hit hard
32 Tasmanian seaport
34 ___ of the Americas, abbr.
35 Cover story
36 Leader
38 Cookbook phrase
39 "_____ are the apple of my eye"
40 Confusing communications
46 Lab eggs
47 Downtime
48 Applaud
49 Phone number, abbr.
50 U.S.N.A. grad, abbr.
51 Looking like certain trees

Down

1 Dom demanded to be called this
2 Dig up
3 Would contraction
4 Twangy, as a voice
5 Draft
6 Positive or negative particle
7 Dog of mixed breed
8 Kenyan people
9 Outrage
10 Old salt
15 Place
16 Feeling isolated
19 Masseur's workplace, maybe
20 Chocolate-flavored coffee
21 Laud
23 Military force
24 Way off base
26 Bug killer, now banned, abbr.
28 Black
29 Theseus abandoned her
31 Messrs.
33 Having two centers
36 Boxer or chow, for example
37 Weight measure
39 Barks
40 Witty remark
41 _____ seen worse!
42 _____ Antonio
43 _____ mine!
44 Escape
45 Company mole

66

99 Shades of Play

Across

1 It grows on you
5 _____ rather do it himself
8 Carol contraction
11 Part of a pot
12 Needle case
14 Grate on
15 Upgraded lashes
17 Period in time
18 Retro
20 Throng
23 Off-color
25 Finnish person
26 One kind of ball
30 Lyrical lines
31 Maria Callas songs
32 Pin down
33 Everyone's after me feeling
35 "To thine own _____ be true"
36 Means of control
37 Hair look
38 Import/export comparison
42 NY time, for short
44 Nips in bed
48 Gaudy scarf
49 Come from
50 Nonexistent
51 One of Greyhound's fleet
52 "Star Trek" rank, abbr.
53 Prize since 1949

Down

1 Meat for a sub
2 Literary collection
3 The state of things intro
4 Get back
5 Zebra clan
6 Flight data, briefly
7 The Everly Brothers composition
8 Sea coast
9 It's the subject of 1099s, abbr.
10 Blue stuff
13 Romantic affairs
16 European peak
19 Hilo garland
20 Icky stuff
21 Spidey sense
22 Theatrical productions
24 Training routine
26 Relative (sl.)
27 Three
28 Shaver
29 Buck
31 Records
34 Show
35 Ready for the dom's activities, perhaps
37 "Collateral" car
39 Lavish affection (on)
40 Flat
41 Beauties
42 Recede
43 Paltry amount
45 Just one antacid
46 Nightmarish street
47 Tricky

67

99 Shades of Play

Across

1 Driver's licenses, etc.
4 Barb
9 Touch-down estimate for "Charlie Tango," abbr.
12 Whisper to your lover
13 Tennis great Rod
14 Testing ground
15 Former name of Tokyo
16 Tree resin used in varnishes and perfumery
17 _____ in good time
18 No mush, stick to the whip
21 _____ before beauty
22 Good name, for short
23 Scads
26 Out-and-out
30 Aspen comparable
31 Brainchild
32 Sweater
35 Frappe
37 It's cut and dried
38 Poetic contraction
39 There's something kinky behind these grins
46 CD's partner, abbr.
47 People at the auction
48 Serpent's temptee
49 Finish, with "up"
50 Advised, old word
51 Compete with a rival
52 Hideout
53 Whodunit, for example
54 Austrian peak

Down

1 Chilled down the tea
2 Extinct bird
3 Procrastinator's promise
4 Heavy hammer
5 Auras
6 Declare
7 Bones
8 A polymer
9 Joie de vivre
10 Baby powder
11 Up to it
19 Old cry from an English fox-hunt
20 Deductive
23 In vitro items
24 Sculler's need
25 Can be archeological
27 Axelike tool
28 Miss-named
29 Go brown
33 L.A. baseball players
34 Embroidery hole
35 Rankle
36 Fix
39 Rubbish
40 Wine they drank on the boat
41 Foreboding sign
42 She warbles about white flags
43 Vale (anagram)
44 Nefarious
45 Escape, in a way

68

99 Shades of Play

Across

1 Broke the limit during the chase
5 Poke fun at
8 Word with room and wear
12 Bear constellation
13 Risk punishment
14 Hero type
15 With no categorization, for short
16 Low
17 Columbus's transport
18 Seizing an advantage
21 Hankering
22 Flurry
23 Cried and cried, post punishment
26 Virgin, for example
30 Compass direction, abbr.
31 Sort
32 What the car chase sparked off
36 Talk excessively
39 Drench
40 Does it really come before beauty?
41 Showing too much, like the blue blouse
47 Shaving stuff
48 Arrest
49 Physical location
51 Children's story start
52 Pitcher's performance gauge, abbr.
53 Tops
54 Fortune-teller
55 Plunder
56 Vientiane is its capital

Down

1 Total
2 Goody-goody
3 To be, to Brutus
4 Ptero_____ (flying dinosaur)
5 Prompt
6 An _____ will
7 Sturdy work boot
8 Bit of bait
9 Publishing activity
10 Continuing after the safe word, e.g.
11 It wasn't just on the wrist!
19 Ball holder
20 "_____ to Billie Joe"
23 _____ canto
24 Daw's cousin
25 Fly catcher
27 Baby wear
28 Unwell
29 Survive, just
33 Same elements, different atom arrangements
34 Wear
35 Intro
36 Tree with gourdlike fruit
37 Back when
38 Come about
41 Alien spacecrafts, abbr.
42 Nothing
43 Freshwater carp
44 Root
45 Star turn
46 Photo-shoot repeat
50 Obstinate animal

69

Across

1 Maître d's offering
5 Betrayer
8 Backing
11 Russia's _____ Mountains
12 Ordinal suffix
13 Burn
14 Hissy fit
15 Adversary
16 Red Room of Pain option
17 Eventually the kid flew it around the Christmas tree!
20 Spoil to an extent
21 Saw
24 Female former enslaver
28 Tasteful watch
30 Bird that doesn't fly
31 Insidious
33 Nothing
34 Chicken
37 Toy dog
40 Dark brown
42 Herbie, e.g.
43 Stockings to turn him on
48 Star followers
51 Sprinkle
52 The first meson discovered
53 A coalition
54 Needle hole
55 Tropical fruit
56 Appropriate
57 He provided good advice
58 Splendor

Down

1 Cornmeal loaf
2 Fish-feeding eagle
3 Fasten
4 Occurring the month before
5 Turns over a new leaf
6 Over
7 Sorority letter
8 Split soup
9 Skedaddled
10 Mineral
13 Beat it
18 Cylinder with reciprocating motion
19 Tol and Alfr ending
22 Heredity factor
23 Auspices (var.)
24 Old EU organization, abbr.
25 Time for a tree for the blip when he grew up
26 Gull
27 Tree
29 Inn serving
32 Participated in America's Cup
35 Some nerve
36 Health org., abbr.
38 Musical-scale note
39 Foil
41 Acted as a ringer
44 "Naked Maja" painter
45 Computer rule of bad input, bad output (sl.)
46 Kind of oak
47 Cut a little
48 Wharton grad, abbr.
49 Matterhorn, e.g.
50 Purchased

70

Across

1 Kind of spirit
5 Café alternative
8 Porcino
11 "_____, Baker, Charlie"
12 Sword handle
14 Don't just seem
15 Dom's attitude
17 Girl's palindromic name
18 Computer accessory
20 Take back, in a way
23 Archipelago member
25 Split
26 First-date reactions
29 Wizard
30 Watch holder
31 Pressure meas., abbr.
33 Fine-tune
35 Rock rich in silicon
36 Decorative case
37 33 and 45 material
38 Characters
42 Ogle
44 Magical means of tying someone up
48 Drink with jam and bread
49 A whole bunch
50 Lover boy
51 Outmoded, with been
52 Insecticide, abbr.
53 Air

Down

1 19th Greek letter
2 Go back
3 Bass, for one
4 Half man, half fish
5 You, in Shakespeare
6 Catcall
7 Other
8 Tenpin alternative
9 Hurler's stat., abbr.
10 Montblanc, e.g.
13 Keyboard operator
16 "Whew!"
19 Pale
20 America's letters, abbr.
21 Mother of pearl
22 Climbing garden plants
24 Paper
26 Victoria's Secret item
27 Gloss or stick
28 Purpose
30 Bullet sounds
32 Calamity
34 Take to court
35 Goes with Madre
37 Drum
39 Auction cry
40 Kind of column
41 "Macbeth" soup with eye of _____
42 Numerical ending
43 Word of success!
45 Slip in a pot, abbr.
46 Mixed-breed dog
47 Mauna _____

71

Across

1 Vertical support of a circular staircase
6 Silklike fabric
11 Sarcastic
13 Hut material
14 Romance at the dry cleaners?
16 Circumference segment
17 Car with a bar
21 Cousin of calypso
22 Young chap
25 Breakdown of social norms
27 In a _____ of her own
30 Shaved alternative
31 Bananalike plant
32 Faucet
34 Rank modifier
35 Twinings was a favorite
36 I found out!
38 _____ said, the better
39 Heart of something
40 Stalk, mobilely
49 Provide, as with some quality
50 Goes away
51 Ogler
52 It all goes back to sex guy

Down

1 Take a quick bite
2 Deviate
3 Suffering
4 Naval rank, abbr.
5 Fleur-de-_____
6 Enfant terrible
7 Promotional efforts
8 Pronoun
9 Waist sash
10 After expenses
12 Go after
15 Grate
17 Statutes
18 Incompetent
19 Cheekiness
20 Watch brand
22 Tag
23 Desert plant
24 Italian commanders
26 Wedding words
28 Place for a stud or a nibble
29 Dines
33 Cargo ship
34 Noisy confusion
37 "Come again?"
40 Yearling sheep
41 DNA's relative, abbr.
42 Cutting tool
43 Ball director
44 Game arbiter
45 Auto
46 Time before
47 Romanian monetary unit
48 Former British money, abbr.

72

99 Shades of Play

Across

1 Uproar
5 Broadcasting overseer, for short
8 Fascinated by
12 Test version
13 "I knew it!"
14 Roulette color
15 Don't treat me as an object!
18 Remote in manner
19 Birth related
22 Chessman
25 "C'est la vie"
26 Place for a chaste kiss
27 Baby blotter
28 Put down
30 Sun, poetically
32 Mischief maker
34 Greek earth goddess (var.)
35 Old-time water-drawing device
36 Irritated
37 Does it really make the heart grow fonder?
40 Did in the manner of Alec in "Tess"
46 The start of little blip
47 Ballad's end
48 Big Dipper
49 Gets hitched
50 Ironic
51 Livens (up)

Down

1 Intelligence agency, abbr.
2 Meadow
3 Store convenience, for short
4 Endangered animals
5 Saturated substances
6 It could be live, online
7 Appetizers
8 Foot part
9 Discouraging words
10 Place for a clasp
11 Uneaten morsel
16 OPEC concern
17 Japanese cartoon
19 Catch red-handed
20 Adjust
21 Outside hard limits
23 Disguise
24 Goosebump raising
26 Brownish color
28 "CSI" accused's defense
29 Prejudiced
31 "___ to the bone"
33 Romantic composer
34 Matured
36 Frigid
38 Decorative pitcher
39 ___ a soul
40 Reporter's question
41 Welcome, Maria!
42 Fizzle
43 Intense anger
44 Rx, abbr.
45 Partakes of

73

Across

1 Weight
5 Fund-raising grp., abbr.
8 Computer freak
12 Hokkaido native
13 Unbroken series
14 _____ the rainbow
15 Grandmothers
16 Frequently, in poetry
17 Ancient writings
18 Issue the realtor had to fix
21 There was a big one over the blip
22 Slippery creature
23 Carefree
25 Ball game on the Med.
28 Aegean Sea island
31 Hold
32 Noah's boat
33 Sodium, e.g.
37 Heavy, of soil
40 Were you _____ it?
41 Make public
42 Homo sapiens
44 Place to get into some pool
49 Language of Lahore
51 Zero
52 Hence
53 One thing philosophers ponder on
54 Walking-only bird
55 Unload, as stock
56 Send to the canvas (sl.)
57 Scale notes
58 Pigeon-_____

Down

1 Ring
2 Iranian coin
3 The "I" of "The King and I"
4 Shellfish
5 Loiters about
6 Calcite rock
7 Deer headgear
8 Remembrance Day mo., abbr.
9 Unremarkable
10 Change the decor
11 Attraction
19 Anthem's fifth word
20 _____-di-dah
24 The way I said
25 Snake
26 Tawny, for example
27 Nastily
29 Heretofore
30 Shade of blue
34 Used before a vowel
35 Tennis maneuver
36 Sillier
37 Hardened blister
38 Sue Grafton's "_____ for Lawless"
39 There was one after the ransom-demand bust
42 Scent
43 Acreage
45 Fruit
46 Creme cookie
47 Check out
48 Jello frame
50 Sky craft, abbr.

74

Across

1 Father's initial emotion when told about little blip
4 Express thoughtful hesitation
7 True love, as in "The Philadelphia Story"
10 Mature
11 "So long!"
12 Paranormal ability, abbr.
13 Style of music
14 With violet or conservative
16 Skye cap
17 Make domination go faster
20 Get bitter about
21 Luau souvenir
22 Back home for good, abbr.
24 Gal of song
26 Burn a bit
30 Copper or bronze
31 Blood classification system
32 Kind of trip
33 Yield
35 Old-time dads
36 Jab
37 Hair, generally
39 It makes one hot
40 Not always resuscitation
46 Kind of jacket
47 Coronet
48 Settle a debt
49 Sharp tool
50 Paper purchase
51 Hackneyed
52 Driver's aid

53 Pipe bend
54 Formerly known as

Down

1 Cleopatra's love, Antony
2 Thickener
3 Left
4 Handle
5 S.A.T. section
6 Cherries
7 Himalayan legend
8 Quickly, quickly, abbr.
9 Motor abbr.
11 Salad veggie
15 Leave speechless
18 Ruminate chew
19 Sot's sound
22 "Arabian Nights" bird
23 Shortly before
24 Deep-blue jewel
25 Bank routing no., abbr.
27 Right after this
28 Back in time
29 Reel's partner
34 Outback runner
36 Authority
38 Canadian city, abbr.
39 Mosque prayer leader
40 Constructed
41 Overflow
42 Far East weight measure
43 Toothpaste, with B
44 Whopper
45 Jekyll's alter ego
46 Rug used in a bathroom

75

Across

1 Fly high
5 Nile viper
8 Collector's goal
11 Barely beat
12 Low
13 Spanish artist, Joan
14 Metal necklace
15 Right-angle extension
16 Popular cookie
17 Aspen transport
20 School group, abbr.
21 Chowed down
24 Billionaire's briefs, doggie style
27 Approval
28 Sweet potato
29 Mountain shoe
31 Nags
35 Attic
38 Stock
39 Don't waste
40 Aspen action
45 Sea foam
48 Aquarium denizen
49 Yucca's kin
50 Consort of Aphrodite
51 Was on the bottom
52 Threshold
53 Word with loose or back
54 Encouraging word
55 Sentry or sub's cry

Down

1 Badger's tunnel
2 Pervasive quality
3 Mogul empire capital
4 Formula
5 Cells in the sea
6 Individual parts
7 Dances
8 Madam's mate
9 Long intro
10 "_____ Hot to Handle," '38 film
13 Walk in leisurely fashion
18 Paper size, abbr.
19 Captain's prediction, abbr.
22 Old Russia, abbr.
23 Prod
24 One _____ one
25 Home to Honolulu
26 Present time
30 _____ takes two to tango
32 Chokers
33 Mate
34 Most foxy
35 Jury verdict, maybe
36 Chucklehead
37 Go over again after the game
41 Foreboding
42 Pelvic bones
43 Coach, Chuck
44 Moola
45 Envelope that comes back
46 Ashes holder
47 Sunset color

76

Across

1 Milky gem
5 Disobedient
8 Sound boomerang
12 Learning style
13 Poem of praise
14 Weatherman's forecast
15 Online diary
16 Berate
18 Orally experienced individual
20 Pacific Ocean fish
21 Physician and vet, for example
23 Italian-sauce origin
27 Confederate soldier, for short
29 She was part of a "bed in" for peace
30 Obviously surprised
33 Metal-bearing rock
34 Helping hand
35 Place for the billionaire to fly off the handle
37 Small gull
40 White, in prescriptions
41 Yielding to the editor
46 Networks
48 East Indian sauce
50 "Argo" setting
51 Money cup
52 Dublin's location
53 Sots' spots
54 Body mark
55 Make fun of

Down

1 Eyeball
2 Politicians, for short
3 Building block of the universe
4 Smooth, musically
5 Fleeing
6 Fall guy
7 CD of unknown
8 Muse of erotic poetry
9 Whip that makes money
10 Attain
11 The loneliest number
17 Stage of bloom
19 Shankar lilt
22 Buona _____
23 Fancy neckwear
24 Focused on something
25 Navigational aid
26 Spa sound
28 Four-poster, e.g.
31 Agricultural worker
32 Wings
36 Footnote word
38 Decayed city
39 "30 Rock" network
42 Mongrel
43 Necroph____
44 Buckeye State
45 Undercover agent
46 Kid
47 Gothic, for one
49 Netherlands river

77

Across

1 Musher's transport
5 Dress (up)
8 School group, abbr.
11 Created
12 Source of iron
13 Podded veggies
14 Like sabotaging "Charlie Tango"
15 Prerequisite in Tokyo
16 Word of honor
17 Post-fight tears
20 Japanese-food fish
21 Stand
24 Pasta cooking standard
28 Arab republic
30 The Smothers Brothers, e.g.
31 The lady's
33 "Poison _____," Coasters song
34 Upbraid for disobeying the dom
37 Characterized by motion
40 African pen
42 Boulder/Coolidge
43 Club dance offender
48 Wind instrument
51 Spanish for sun
52 "The Picture of Dorian _____"
53 Frame of a ship
54 Night before
55 Rockefeller Center attraction
56 Unmatching
57 Cool in the '80s
58 Dexterity

Down

1 Kin of merganser
2 Hot rock
3 Adjust
4 Cross out
5 What bitch troll did with the kid
6 Nabisco brand
7 Variety
8 Pot-pie morsel
9 Body mark
10 Silvery gray
13 Search party
18 Maintained
19 The beginning of kooky
  and kinky
22 Let out
23 _____ Strauss
24 Infomercials, for example
25 Fortune
26 The playroom's was usually
  locked
27 "Omigod!"
29 Big Apple initials
32 Spread throughout
35 Pigeonhole
36 Spicy stew
38 Scold
39 Certain settler
41 Short-straw drawer
44 Astronomical sighting
45 Puccini solo
46 Tandoor breads
47 Kindergartner
48 "Well, lookee here!"
49 Pal
50 Getting on

78

99 Shades of Play

Across

1 Therefore
5 Fond du _____
8 Jezebel's idol
12 Traveler
13 Relative of an ostrich
14 What's more
15 Order to overzealous smoochers
17 Store sect., abbr.
18 Vehement disapproval
20 Burn with steam
23 Permitted
26 Slime
27 Needing one of two things
28 Dynamite, abbr.
29 Midsection
31 Basic metal
33 Dissuades
35 _____ I didn't know!
36 Drink
37 Ready for action
38 Hero of "The Arabian Nights"
41 Still-life subject
44 Late-night Aspen action
48 Drive-_____, abbr.
49 Sky
50 Encircle
51 Milit. rank, abbr.
52 Hot spring
53 Continental currency

Down

1 Instigate
2 _____ v. Wade
3 Grasp
4 Database solutions provider
5 Boxer, Spinks
6 Old Testament book
7 Form of cloud showing vertical development
8 Rotten apple
9 Lager
10 Venom carrier
11 Great deal
16 Checkers color
19 Ripped
20 Big drinker
21 Complex unit
22 New Mexico city
24 Stopped lying
25 Song element
27 Towel stitching
29 Mark on the skin
30 Pain-reliever plants
32 Newt
34 Get emotional
35 Fit for farming
37 Wane
39 Image on a radar screen
40 That certain something
41 List, abbr.
42 Mega rock group
43 Wander off course
45 Debt letters
46 Part of Scandinavia, abbr.
47 Federal agency, abbr.

79

99 Shades of Play

Across

1 Catchall, abbr.
5 Cups the billionaire played with
8 17th letter of the Greek alphabet
11 "Tosca" tune
12 Not be up-to-date
13 Very, very long time
14 _____, repent at leisure
17 Animation
18 Bronze, for one
19 Confused
22 Better than tearful
26 Unlikely story
30 Holier-than-__
31 Jedi, first name
32 Shorthand pro, abbr.
34 It fits in a lock
35 Yearn
37 Suspect
39 Company symbols
41 Tips
42 Understand
44 Got a send-off with rice
45 Make an aural advance
51 Before, of yore
52 _____ all in a day's work. . . .
53 Square
54 Conger is one
55 Radio dash
56 Its motto is "Lux et veritas"

Down

1 Mayan language
2 Bank offering, for short
3 Knight title
4 Type of pistil
5 Baby indicator
6 Dashed
7 Turkish military leader
8 Begrudge
9 Angry
10 Single
15 "The Second Coming" poet
16 Marauding Khan
19 Island of coral, ring shaped
20 Verboten
21 Highball
23 Evil spirit
24 Really let have it
25 Portable domed dwellings
27 Kind of card, abbr.
28 Hula hoop
29 Starfleet Academy grad., abbr.
33 Glossy brown fur
36 Creed
38 Turtle
40 Expanse
43 Camelot character
44 Make bubbles
45 Previously named
46 Outrage
47 When plane is expected, abbr.
48 Gametes
49 Sound unit
50 Mariner's point, abbr.

80

99 Shades of Play

Across

1 Brother of Cain
5 Weekend getaway
8 Small screen item that became a big deal
12 Area in Germany
13 Migratory fish
14 City north of Carson City
15 Stride
16 Latte ingredient
18 Arctic look
20 Boiled buckwheat
22 Place
26 Day before
27 Staff leader
30 Tinted
31 Kind of part
32 Gold measurement
34 License-plate sticker
35 With no delay, abbr.
37 Stay hygienic
38 Casan follower
39 Ali and Tyson
41 A wheat
43 Bone-marrow disease
46 Billonaire being pensive, after fight
49 Proton's place
52 Raise Cain
53 Outer garment
54 Inner goddess's possessive cry, "He's _____!"
55 Military leader
56 It's often sloppy
57 Picture

Down

1 Cleopatra's killer?
2 Plaintive cry
3 Levy on sales
4 Healing worm, supposedly
5 Time periods, abbr.
6 Fertilizer fuel
7 Leguminous plants
8 Opening
9 Hawaiian necklace
10 Wayside stop
11 Horror writer
17 Moving to and _____
19 Talk, talk, talk
20 Meat on a stick
21 Dispatch boat
23 Easier than stick shift
24 Buzz off
25 J. _____
28 Causes
29 Cambrian, for one
33 1969 Oates novel
36 Ball game
40 Wine choice
42 U.S. coastal resort
44 Feeling there is a _____ in your stomach
45 Like custard
46 La Perla offering
47 Improvise
48 Bed cry
50 Beatles collaborator
51 Demographic segment

81

99 Shades of Play

Across

1 Dull sound
5 Media outlet
8 Frisk, with "down"
11 Detest
12 In the open
13 Foreshadow
14 One of seven, abbr.
15 Pitching measure, abbr.
16 Literary _____
17 Inscrutible
20 Floral ring
21 Pores over Thomas Hardy
24 Bony fish
28 Star turn
29 In-vitro items
30 Expression of disapproval
32 Schuss
34 Party times
37 Cool in the '90s
40 Lowest point
42 Musical gift
43 Instrument to play on
48 Experienced
51 Prefix, recent
52 Give the cold shoulder
53 Turn
54 Gew-_____, trinket
55 Dirt
56 Quiche ingredient
57 Sea eagle
58 _____ word

Down

1 In this way
2 Metal fastener
3 Four Corners state
4 Desecrate
5 Live peacefully together
6 It's used as veneer
7 Way up or down
8 Luau serving
9 Rumpus
10 Ring count
13 Dim from tears
18 Prefix with colonial
19 N.Z. parrot
22 Gossip
23 South American monkey
24 "Love _____ Love You Baby"
25 Tied up
26 Volcanic flow
27 Spa spot
31 Get the cuffs in place
33 Stylish
35 Trimmer
36 Knighted one
38 Make use of
39 Little blip brought one to a head
41 Kitchen appliance
44 Close in on
45 Tolstoy's Karenina
46 _____ said
47 Wind up on stage
48 Fifth, e.g., abbr.
49 Plead
50 Pull his _____

82

99 Shades of Play

Across

1 Varnish substance
4 Bulgarian cash
7 Salon stuff
10 Approval
11 Led Zeppelin album
12 Charles or Romano
13 Room for the dom
16 Adjusting exactly
17 Onion-flavored roll
20 Tongue-lashing
24 Pool agitation
25 Cuffs, metal
27 Zip
28 Group of three
29 Animal nose
30 Making the biggest racket
32 Adorable
33 Preserve
34 Sorrow
35 Sea litter
38 Ocular trapping
42 Seafood selection
43 Tumult
44 Make lovey-dovey talk
45 Capitol Hill vote
46 Decompose
47 Hog haven

Down

1 On the ___
2 Ottoman officer
3 Expensive
4 In _____ of (place of)
5 James Joyce country
6 Tourist
7 Palm with a spiny trunk
8 Have
9 Soap ingredient
14 Taste
15 Come together
17 East Indian herb
18 Expression
19 Improvise
21 Cancel
22 Because of
23 Glowing remnant
25 Bicuspid
26 Portuguese airport, abbr.
28 Cashboxes
31 Using protection
32 Newspaper feature
34 Mail boat
36 List for the day
37 Edinburgh local
38 Dusk, to Donne
39 Sure!
40 _____ only that
41 Gentile

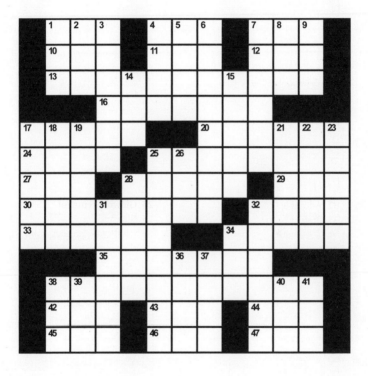

83

99 Shades of Play

Across

1 Some are erogenous
6 Brit media, abbr.
9 Horse food
12 Sidestep
13 Beam
14 New Year's _____
15 Pine exudation
16 Pendulum's path
17 Wonderland drink
18 Doggone control freak keeps you _____
21 Physics lawmaker
22 Poet's "before"
23 Trophy for a matador
26 Thing, in law
27 R & B singer, India._____
30 Window-shop
32 Vend again
34 Wild party
35 Cries when a hard limit is crossed
36 Caribou kin
37 Seafood delicacy
39 Baseball Hall of Famer, Mel
40 What are you doing with those paddles?
47 Choose
48 Cow sound
49 Eagle's nest
50 Busy one
51 It may be bruisable
52 Thick outer coat of a seed
53 Climactic shout

54 Silently agree
55 Suit material, following poly

Down

1 Tolerance level
2 Kind of mitt
3 Astronaut's org., abbr.
4 Censor
5 They are older
6 Romantic composer
7 San Francisco rail system, abbr.
8 Revolution
9 Roman mistresses
10 Madison and Fifth, abbr.
11 "Sure"
19 Liquid butter
20 Generations
23 Sink
24 Constellation near Scorpius
25 Rose-shaped badges
28 Unhealthy
29 Comics cry
31 _____ the appetite . . .
32 Military training org., abbr.
33 One who loves beauty
35 Lacking worth
38 Threshold
40 Pass
41 Olympic blade
42 What the safe word means
43 Flirtation devices
44 Previously
45 High flier
46 Four quarters

84

99 Shades of Play

Across

1 On vacation
5 100 lbs., abbr.
8 Hot casino destination in China
10 Joined by a common cause
13 Mooring sites
14 Blabbed secret info
15 Crazy like the marquis
18 Fiddler's place
19 Mischief maker
24 Coffee fave, made by secretary
29 They're getting money
30 Velvetlike fabric
31 Watch present from London
32 Easing of strained relations
33 French door part
35 In which, he doesn't know whether he's coming or going
43 Trojan hero
44 Out-and-out
46 Night flight
47 Parisian subway
48 Curtain holder
49 Fashion

Down

1 Electric-guitar hookup
2 Destined for a foster home
3 Winged fruit shrub
4 Quick and nimble
5 Dressed
6 Collaborative Web site
7 Golf-ball props
9 Olympics chant, abbr.
10 Plus
11 Flyer
12 Herbicide, abbr.
16 _____ Kringle
17 Hither and _____
19 Printing office, abbr.
20 Computer capacity, abbr.
21 Get a load of
22 "French Kiss" star
23 Extra 24 hours in February
25 Stout relative
26 Oodles
27 Egyptian king, for short
28 Before, to Byron
30 Flying formations
32 Kind of fingerprint, abbr.
34 Basilica part
35 Musical notes segment
36 Look of lust
37 _____nesian
38 Call for
39 The total of something
40 Romantic couple
41 German name
42 Computer whiz
45 Lobster eggs

85

99 Shades of Play

Across

1 Archeological find
5 Get ready to flee from the Dodge
8 Cotswold cry
11 Allege as fact (law)
12 Jungle swinger
13 Lung, for a fish
14 Guru
15 Perfect rating
16 Space
17 Got ready for a fight
20 Lady deer
21 Johnson work
22 Diminisher
25 Unkempt
29 Applesauce
30 Pub offering
31 Sherbet fruit
35 Hawk
38 Key word for a dom
39 Deserve punishment
40 Sartorial item for the playroom
47 Medicinal berry
48 Physics unit
49 Small amount
50 Ella Fitzgerald subject
51 Hawaiian wreath
52 Old west gun
53 Course setting, abbr.
54 Court cry
55 Some pipes

Down

1 Toiletry item
2 Football
3 Cultural imitation
4 West German politician
5 Somewhat
6 Cutlass
7 Seller
8 Life summaries
9 "Thanks _____!"
10 Donations
13 "Holberg Suite" composer
18 Loving call
19 Government group monitoring food and drugs, abbr.
22 _____ wrestle
23 Stole
24 Mechanical money dispenser, abbr.
26 _____pole
27 Nothing but
28 Gravity-force letter
32 Feature
33 Farm female
34 Sign up for college
35 Allow
36 It's full of periods
37 Very cold material
40 Markdown
41 Superstar
42 Bathe
43 Indian dish, ingredient
44 Whip, in a way
45 Common contraction
46 Snacks

86

99 Shades of Play

Across

1 Bluenose
5 Girl from Ipanema town
8 Pound (down)
12 Ambience
13 Recipe word
14 Large lake
15 Family folk
16 Pinky
17 Give way on
18 Strand to be put in place
21 Chinese dynasty
22 A Bobbsey twin
23 Crying like a goat
26 Places to sit
30 "_____ true!"
31 Christened
32 Interest
36 Way to take your tea
39 Confidant
40 World power, abbr.
41 Sign of supreme happiness
48 Ill-mannered boor
49 Zilch
50 Be hopping mad
51 45th admitted state
52 "You don't say!"
53 Holds
54 Rank
55 Misjudge
56 Water-skiing locale

Down

1 Agreement
2 Hold sway over
3 Persia, now
4 One of the most successful
 protesters of the 20th century
5 Credit standing
6 Very popular star
7 Greek theaters
8 Music at the club
9 Territory
10 Certain skirt
11 One may exert pressure
19 Hightailed it
20 Lucrative
23 Chest protector
24 Broke bread
25 Silver-gray color
27 Lennon's lady
28 Romanian currency
29 Good to go
33 Impassiveness
34 Murphy's _____
35 Pipe collar
36 Billionaire's man Friday
37 Dummy
38 Play
41 Pouring sound
42 Tiny amount
43 One of the Marianas
44 Cake level
45 Corn Belt state
46 Connection
47 Different

1	2	3	4		5	6	7		8	9	10	11
12					13				14			
15					16				17			
18				19				20				
		21				22						
23	24	25				26				27	28	29
30									31			
32			33	34	35		36	37	38			
		39				40						
41	42	43			44				45	46	47	
48				49				50				
51				52				53				
54				55				56				

99 Shades of Play

Across

1 Applaud
5 Winter-sport action
8 Finishes off
12 Locks
13 Relative
14 Spiced stew
15 Watch the gorgeous one take a shower
18 Gull cry
19 Bass _____
20 Mischievous fairies
23 Vernacular
26 Roman 7
27 Billionaire's peers
28 German spa
29 Fern-to-be
31 Vowel for Plato
33 Bitch troll's plaything
35 Beer holder
36 Milk dippers
37 Persian Gulf port
39 Watch a baby
40 Add
41 Hand that won't stay still
48 1973 Supreme Court decision name
49 Reproductive cells
50 Place
51 Stink
52 Edible mushroom
53 Hypothetical form of matter

Down

1 Dance, when doubled
2 Young 'un
3 Point
4 Choice
5 Throw off
6 Equipment
7 Breathing device
8 Witch groupings
9 40 Thieves leader, Baba
10 Kind of chart
11 Farm female
16 Thing, legally
17 Top-notch
20 Role in Haydn's "The Creation"
21 No-man's-land
22 Sun shade
24 Eggheads
25 Aquatic mammal
27 Rapture
29 Impassive
30 Formulated after the fact (Latin)
32 Palindromic title
34 Prefix with day or year
37 Virus
38 Abundantly
40 Like some decisions
41 Low card
42 Roll of dough
43 Repeats five times in an ABBA song
44 Contraction
45 Afflict
46 Wranglers alternative
47 Colorful flower, for short

88

99 Shades of Play

Across

1 Light greenish-blue
5 Smidgen
8 Great Lakes fish
12 Presses for payment
13 Before, in verse
14 Undercooked
15 Teenage problems
16 Put on
17 Wild revelry
18 Irresistible
21 Yo-ho-ho drink
22 It's a scream
23 Perk up your ears
26 Made a throaty sound
30 Flood escape vessel
31 Drink fave
32 Strange bird
36 Bondage
39 Go public with
40 Freelancer's enc., abbr.
41 "Don't push me on this" look
46 Edge
47 Anthem contraction
48 Schusser's support
50 50-50
51 Garland flowers
52 Outstanding
53 She's quoted in a gift from the billionaire
54 Emergency group, abbr.
55 Popular jeans

Down

1 Woodworking tool
2 Throw in the towel
3 Biblical preposition
4 Categorize
5 Wish harm upon
6 Fairway club
7 Sore
8 Criminals
9 Damage
10 Push for
11 Ottoman governor
19 Appearance
20 Green color
23 Bar topic
24 Displeasure
25 Hit the slopes
27 Ed. group, abbr.
28 Wriggler
29 Lentil sauce
33 Black birds
34 Expire
35 American songbird
36 Trouble, in Yiddish
37 WWII general, Arnold
38 Leased home
41 Buckle
42 15th or 13th day, Roman
43 Overflow
44 Slender instrument
45 Draw to a close
46 Firm
49 Court matter

89

Across

1 Woodstock gear
5 Election winners
8 Hardly thrilling
12 Bank transaction
13 Romanian money
14 Bug
15 Sexual manual
18 Kind of patch
19 Iniquity arena
20 Fairer sex
23 Kind of gun
26 Commotions
27 A support for something
29 "Just kidding!"
30 Arouse desire
31 Kim follower
33 Meals
35 This, _____, and the other
36 Swagger
37 Handed out cards
38 Decide
39 Stocking's end
40 Dom's order on "Star Wars"?
47 Cleaning bar
48 Call to Bo Peep
49 Like some china
50 Soft stroke
51 Wander off course
52 Greek-salad cheese

Down

1 Mont Blanc, e.g.
2 Farm remark
3 Dance step
4 Attacks with words
5 Hip bones
6 "The Matrix" character
7 Summer girl's wear
8 West German politician
9 Pouting area
10 Tongue loosener
11 Pronoun
16 Ring count
17 NH airport
20 Peaked
21 Aromas
22 Bach composition
24 Hello or good-bye
25 Kidney related
27 Lab item
28 Maze animal
30 Brownish gray
32 The Little Giant
34 Immediate
35 Irritate
37 A dwarf
39 Boris, for one
40 Recipe amt., abbr.
41 Marker letters
42 Absorb, as a cost
43 Golfer's goal
44 Come in equal
45 Explosive stuff, abbr.
46 Senate declaration

90

99 Shades of Play

Across

1 Desolate
5 Manhandle
8 Final notice, abbr.
12 Rajah's wife
13 Peruvian tuber
14 Normal prefix
15 Excited with anticipation
16 Crew member
17 "Ah, gosh!"
18 Provocative
21 Keats's forte
22 Group of mountain nymphs
24 Like a rainbow
27 Power
28 Long March leader
29 Administer
30 Bard's nightfall
32 Marquis follower
35 Bungle
37 Aircraft
38 Hoodwink
39 Like sex with a dom
44 It could be wicked. . . .
46 Playing hard to get
47 Cream ingredient
48 Pub purchase
49 Et cetera
50 Stand up
51 Dom's expectation
52 A whiskey
53 Time pieces

Down

1 Annoyance word
2 Melodic Hindu music
3 Ever's partner
4 First body part into the water
5 Dorset port
6 Health-giving berry
7 Area of conflict
8 First act
9 Suitcases
10 Glass, of public radio
11 Bit
19 Make sense, with "up"
20 Hatred
23 Not natural
24 Before noon, abbr.
25 Harsh, grating sound
26 Underground worker's haunt
27 Best guess, abbr.
29 Lemon, sometimes
31 Word of rejection
33 Exquisite
34 B&B
35 Farm noise
36 Private
38 Bonnie's companion
40 Scrawny
41 Pelvic parts
42 Snoopy
43 Turns right
44 Federal printing office, abbr.
45 Kid

91

99 Shades of Play

Across

1 Lemon topping
5 "Be quiet!"
8 Great quantity
12 Arch type
13 Besides
14 Eastern prince
15 Entreaty
16 Long, long time
17 Seattle, for one
18 Parisian site attached to bracelet
21 Darjeeling or oolong
22 Casting requirement
23 Sweet-talk the dom
26 Draw
30 Americ___
31 Type of tripper
32 Vulgar
36 Kitty treat
39 Magical
40 Black-and-tan ingredient
41 Called, when smashed
46 Kind of market
48 Give a hand
49 Prefix with graph
50 Consider
51 ___nky, graceful in movement
52 Olfactory property
53 Batman's Robin
54 Drive obliquely
55 Dry run

Down

1 Handle things
2 Tangerine and grapefruit hybrid
3 Shelf
4 Not listening
5 Funeral stones
6 Cry of derision
7 Awards
8 Ebb
9 Middle Eastern chief
10 Toned
11 Have a go at
19 Slippery one
20 Stir-fry pan
23 Audi, for one
24 Cuckoo bird
25 Shot she forgot
27 Decade
28 Animation platform, abbr.
29 Bell___
33 Lofted house
34 Moldovan moolah
35 Hereditary ruler
36 He deals with a lot of clubs
37 "Aladdin" prince
38 Afternoon affair component
41 Action
42 Metric weight
43 Take on cargo
44 Greek god of love
45 Bull's-eye hitter
46 Organization for health issues, abbr.
47 Orchid arrangement

92

99 Shades of Play

Across

1 If it's cute it's an asset
4 Princess tormentor
7 Griddle
10 Caribbean music
11 Genevan water
12 Brazilian city, familiarly
13 Provocative realtor wear
16 Drink basis
17 OPEC land
20 Loses one's cool
24 Alcoholic beverage
25 Pest that likes humidity
28 Metal
29 Equipped
30 Well-kept secret, for some
31 Warning to seductive realtor
33 Hot blood
34 "Don't get any _____!"
35 Swiss mathematician
37 Arranges the suitcase again
41 Playful flirting touch
45 Bard's preposition
46 Take to court
47 No-goodnik
48 Denouement
49 Wee one
50 Getaway

Down

1 Interview
2 Go downhill fast
3 Pungent
4 Tell it to the judge
5 "My Name Is _____"
6 Have a hankering
7 Home built in a day
8 Plague
9 Rebuffs
14 Rural sight
15 Having hearing projections
17 Police club
18 War story
19 Source of sesame seed
21 Holy _____
22 Tidal flood
23 Navigate
25 Big do
26 Global financial overseer, abbr.
27 Make the calls
29 Valuable
32 Flashed
35 Stretch
36 PC operators
38 Snoop Dogg song
39 Water color
40 Prompted
41 Spelling movie: "Akeelah and the _____"
42 Cremation vase
43 Cook in the microwave
44 Pilot's announcement, abbr.

93

99 Shades of Play

Across

1 Likely
4 Greek vowel
7 Herbal drink, sometimes
10 Conniption fit
11 Query list, for short
12 Matterhorn, e.g.
13 "My body's off limits" order
16 Crowd noises
17 "Aladdin" prince
18 Show off
20 A canonical hour
23 Fathers
24 Dom's requirement for a sub
26 Former South African movement, abbr.
27 Basin
28 Pull on one's heartstrings
30 Amuse oneself
32 Mozart's "L'_____ del Cairo"
33 Out of bed
34 Barbaric
36 Native American people
37 Live wire, so to speak
38 Kinky, kooky, kicking and screaming, etc.
42 A long way
43 "A rat!"
44 Length of life
45 100 lbs., abbr.
46 Cube
47 Plead

Down

1 Relief
2 Large nose
3 Kind of horn
4 Amphibians
5 1985 Rick Springfield album
6 Underwater swimmer
7 Sesame paste
8 Krueger's street
9 Bruiser
14 Pampered one
15 Walk clumsily
18 Mani/pedi place
19 Bamboo eater
21 Followers
22 Dressing
24 Not a bungalow
25 Weathered-hill rock
27 Heavy-coated dog
29 8 pts., abbr.
31 English royal-family line
34 Tent bed
35 Popular celeb destination
37 Barrier in a fairy tale
38 Certain refrigerant, briefly
39 Untouched
40 Chinese calligrapher, Qing
41 Container

94

99 Shades of Play

Across

1 Fat letters
4 As written
7 Get in tune with
11 Fan sound
12 "Much _____ About Nothing"
13 Unfortunate
14 Breakfast fave
17 Curse
18 Pelvic bones
21 Digital research document
25 Contract nondisclosure section, abbr.
26 Cold-cut locale
29 Isaac's eldest
30 Quirky
31 The foiling of the ransom demand became a media _____
33 Women's _____
34 Soul singer, Redding
36 Barely beat
37 Victorian, for one
38 Phony
40 Area of South Africa
42 Crazies
45 A free hand in the Red Room of Pain
50 Double-reed woodwind
51 Third guy with the same name
52 Vacationing
53 One joule per second
54 Rock-climber arena
55 Bag-out order

Down

1 Unit of work
2 Disfigure
3 Lingerie that shows a lot
4 Japanese wine
5 Brief affair
6 Making aboriginal noises
7 Area
8 "_____ Are My Sunshine"
9 Choice word
10 Computer tube, abbr.
15 Sidestep
16 Swindle
18 Be a busybody
19 Enlarge
20 Arabic judge
22 Key
23 Lagos currency
24 Of an underground railway
27 Entirely
28 Called the shots
32 Joint
35 Seven persons
39 "_____ Ta Be My Girl"
41 English race place
43 Muse of history
44 Washing his became quite a performance
45 Unnerve
46 Fabric woven from goat hair
47 Decay
48 Clamor
49 Airline abbreviation

95

99 Shades of Play

Across

1 Sunrise direction
5 Relaxation center
8 Trade
12 Repeat
13 Ping-pong-net skim
14 Drink to excess
15 Nest
16 Wall cover
17 Proclaim
18 Wanting it all the time
21 Everyone is looking for the _____
22 Get under the skin
23 Able to stand up to the dom
26 Bones of noses
30 Barley beard
31 Bread roll
32 Animal similar to the hedgehog
36 Scream _____ murder!
39 WWW address, abbr.
40 Thumbs-up vote
41 Much-loved mojito
45 Trot or canter
47 Note
48 Metrical unit
50 Batman's Robin
51 _____ bono
52 "Way to go!"
53 Produced
54 Put in stitches
55 Itsy-bitsy biter

Down

1 Slippery one
2 Palm species
3 Lower foreleg
4 Some sculptures
5 Granite colored
6 Prefix with scope or meter
7 Get
8 Pursues
9 Manned a loom
10 King Kong, e.g.
11 The "p" in mpg
19 Social insect
20 Lingerie item
23 Kind of cat
24 Lamb's mother
25 Country stopover
27 Blood-classification system, abbr.
28 Young guy
29 Operative
33 Furrowed
34 Slip
35 Buckle hooks
36 Blow _____
37 Bruce of "Dragon" fame
38 Manual motoring
41 Entree add-on
42 Had on
43 Parade stopper
44 Fitness assoc., abbr.
45 Chitchat
46 Brush that blows you away
49 Put one's two cents in

96

Across

1 Furniture wood
4 Special _____
7 Much-desired real-estate vista
10 Fawn's mother
11 Meadow
12 Swiss mountain
13 Hardy's villain in a billionaire's gift
16 Cold War leader
17 Perennial plant
18 Singing groups
21 Distant
25 Fabric collections
26 Certain complex
27 "Mârouf" baritone
28 Bounder
29 Naval rank, abbr.
30 Medieval instrument, like a trombone
33 Elaborate melody
34 Agreement that was never drawn up
35 Buccaneering
37 Hockey great, Bobby
38 Mandela's org., abbr.
39 Goes with taking it off
44 Fish catcher
45 Foot extension
46 Old-time welcome
47 Thickness
48 Stumble
49 Snatch

Down

1 Tack on
2 Symbol of worthlessness
3 Recluse
4 Margarines
5 Each
6 Enjoyed
7 Deli offering
8 Right-angle bend in a pipe
9 Imitate
14 Legal people
15 Decorated, as a cake
18 Fastener
19 Seed scar
20 Drink with rocks
22 "The Barber of Seville"
23 Blouselike garment
24 Thesis
26 Muesli morsel
28 Copper source
31 Difficult, as of a problem
32 Songwriter, Bacharach
33 Mathematical function
35 Cell alternative
36 Bl_____ pancake
39 Econ. indicator, abbr.
40 It can be shocking
41 Easter's beginning
42 Lab eggs
43 State abbreviation

Across

1 Healing sign
5 Soft plug
8 Rat's place
11 Pepsi
12 Wrath
13 It can be drop-down
14 Sunday closing
15 Bust
16 Ends partner
17 Soiree with a dancing auction
20 Slip a cog
21 Healthy red
24 Ruler with a harem
28 Meat on pita
29 Particle
30 _____ bit
32 Also called, abbr.
34 Rapper is one
37 In love, in a big way
40 Kind of ink
42 Excitement
43 Planning something really wicked
48 Match up
51 Latin for eggs
52 Overcast
53 New Zealand evergreen
54 Tennis-court divider
55 Frolic
56 And all that jazz, abbr.
57 Compass point, abbr.
58 Alternatively

Down

1 Swindle
2 Deep sleep
3 Pub stock
4 Provider of the ransom money
5 Row of hay
6 Kuwaiti, e.g.
7 Prevent
8 Chaired
9 "Troilus _____ Cressida," Shakespeare
10 Transport
13 Rancid
18 Pitcher's performance gauge, abbr.
19 Blockhead
22 Expression of annoyance
23 Harness
24 Mathematical number
25 AZ native
26 In the near future
27 Fellows
31 Give out
33 _____ other
35 Draw forth
36 Push over
38 Wedding agreement
39 On-off switch
41 Make reparation
44 Baking chamber
45 Daunting exam
46 Sculls
47 Causeway
48 Mademoiselle
49 At this time
50 "Today" network

99 Shades of Play

Across

1 Compass
5 Computer tube, abbr.
8 _____ Beta Kappa
11 "Rats!"
12 Entice and trap
14 Eats
15 Kind of strap
17 Unit of electrical resistance
18 Knight known for his chivalry
20 A different type of pole
23 Gait faster than a walk
25 Computer proprietor
26 Enchant
29 Silver attire
30 Check endorser
31 Drop the ball
33 Trapped
35 Emmy-winning TV comedy
36 Picnic problem
37 Star, for short
38 Social butterfly
42 Leave dumbstruck
44 Inner-goddess move
48 Kia, for one
49 South American monkey
50 Vice president under Jefferson
51 U.S.N. officer, abbr.
52 Wager
53 Eli home

Down

1 Proclamations
2 Criminal charge
3 Historical period
4 Fisherman
5 Chinese dynasty
6 Officer-commissioning program, abbr.
7 Kind of bag
8 Electric eye
9 "Yeah, right!"
10 Distinctive theory
13 Type of sports shoe
16 Goes with eggs for breakfast
19 Scrap of food
20 Batman foe
21 Weeping willow
22 Youngsters
24 Musketeer number
26 Snare
27 "Beauty is in the _____ of the beholder"
28 Get hitched
30 Endangered animals
32 Southern soldier, abbr.
34 It has moles, abbr.
35 Manages
37 Stick which had many meanings
39 Kuwaiti or Qatari
40 Fire pottery
41 Column in a paper, abbr.
42 Expert flier
43 Haggard
45 In the capacity of
46 Dot-com's address
47 Previous to (prefix)

SOLUTIONS

99 Shades of Play

#1

1F	2A	3S	4T			5B	6I	7Z		8M	9B	10A
11L	I	M	O		12P	O	L	E		13A	L	B
14E	R	I	N		15E	R	I	E		16S	O	B
17D	E	L	I		18D	N	A		19H	O	N	E
	20S	E	C	21U	R	E	D	22B	O	N	D	S
			23Z	O	O		24L	U	R	E	S	
	25O	26R	B	S		27A	E	R	Y			
28T	29E	P	E	E		30E	R	E				
31S	P	A	N	K	32I	N	G	P	33A	34C	35E	
36W	I	L	D		37S	L	Y		38G	A	N	39G
40A	L	I		41P	A	I	L		42I	N	D	O
43N	O	N		44E	A	S	E		45S	T	O	W
46A	G	E		47A	C	T		48T	O	W	N	

#2

1T	E	2A		4C	5F	6C		7A	8R	9I	10A
11N	E	D		12R	I	O		13P	A	I	R
14T	R	Y	15T	O	J	U	16M	P	H	I	M
		17T	O	P	I	C	A	L			
18C	19L	E	A	N			21H	Y	E	22N	23A
24W	O	N		25A	V	I	A	T	O	R	
27M	A	S		28S	C	A	N	S		29N	E	30B
31M	U	32S	T	A	N	G			33O	N	E
34Y	E	M	E	N		35A	36S	S	A	Y	
		37A	T	T	38R	A	C	T			
40R	41O	42L	L	S	H	E	R	E	Y	43E	44S
45E	V	I	L		46U	T	E		47L	E	A
48D	A	D	S		49S	E	A		50E	K	E

#3

1M	A	2R	4L			5B	O	7T		8P	9T	10A
11A	L	E	E		12C	A	V	A		13R	A	N
14L	I	R	A		15O	D	O	R		16O	B	I
17T	B	A	R		18B	E	L		19E	T	A	
	20I	N	N	21E	R	G	O	22D	D	E	S	23S
				24T	A	G		25R	E	A	C	T
26R	E	27A	28C	29H			30A	N	N	O	Y	
31E	N	V	O	Y		32S	33A	W				
34S	C	A	R	L	35E	T	F	L	36U	37S	38H	
	39A	T	E		40R	A	F		41N	A	Y	42S
43A	G	A		44T	U	P	I		45P	U	P	A
46H	E	R		47A	P	E	X		48I	C	O	N
49A	S	S		50I	T	S		51N	E	S	S	

#4

1I	2T	3S		4E	5R	6R		7H	8A	9F	10T
11T	O	T		12R	U	E		13U	N	C	O
14D	O	E	15S	N	T	D	O	16N	I	C	E
		17L	A	S	H	O	U	T			
18R	19O	20S	E	S		21R	E	22T	R	O	
25A	R	M		26S	27L	28E	29W		30D	O	U	R
31I	I	I		32Y	O	K	E	33L		34R	N	A
35N	E	T	36T		37B	E	T	A		38S	O	N
39S	L	E	E	40P			41T	42H	O	N	G
		43E	A	R	44A	45C	46H	E			
47L	I	48T	49T	L	E	P	R	I	N	50C	51E
52A	C	H	E		53N	E	O		54C	A	T
55B	E	E	R		56T	S	P		57E	R	A

#5

1E	G	3O			4O	5P	6T		7S	8P	9A
10N	O	V	11A		12F	A	R	E		13O	A	T
14E	T	A	S		15A	K	I	N		16D	I	E
		17S	18T	R	U	M		19W	A	R	
20N	21I	22N	A	S	I	M	O	23N	E	
24A	C	U	M	E	N		25A	N	26K	27L	28E
29R	O	D		30T	A	31R	32O	T		33E	E	L
34K	N	E	35E	S		36E	M	U		37P	A	S
	38S	E	X	39P	E	R	40T	I	S	E	
41P	42A	P		43E	U	L	E	R			
44S	I	R		45A	B	L	E		46E	47G	48A	49D
50I	S	M		51L	E	S	T		52Y	A	W	N
53T	H	Y		54I	C	E		55S	E	A	

#6

D	I	E	S		K	A	Y			O	B	I
D	I	R	E		E	N	E		K	N	I	T
T	I	E	D	U	P	I	N	K	N	O	T	S
			A	F	T			S	E	E		
	U	N	T	O			N	A	G	S		
F	L	U	E		N	O	O	N	D	A	Y	S
A	C	T		B	I	D	D	Y		B	R	A
D	E	T	A	I	L	E	D		P	L	U	M
	R	Y	A	S			K	E	E	P		
		R	O	D		S	O	L				
U	N	C	O	N	D	I	T	I	O	N	A	L
P	E	O	N		A	R	E		T	A	L	E
S	T	Y			Y	E	W		A	B	L	E

#7

	J	A	R		E	L	M		O	D	O	R
	U	S	E		D	I	E		B	A	B	E
	T	H	O	M	A	S	T	A	L	L	I	S
		P	O	M	P	A	N	O				
J	U	L	E	P			Z	I	N	C	S	
I	R	O	N			G	O	O	G	L	Y	
B	I	D		H	E	M	A	N		O	N	E
	A	G	H	A	S	T			A	N	O	N
	H	E	E	L	S		L	E	E	D	S	
		P	L	E	A	S	E	R				
S	U	B	C	O	N	S	C	I	O	U	S	
O	K	R	A		C	I	A		B	R	O	
B	E	A	T		E	A	R		E	N	D	

#8

G	O	A	D		C	O	P		F	D	A
A	B	L	E		B	O	A		L	E	G
W	O	L	F	I	S	H	S	M	I	L	E
K	E	Y	E	D		S	T	U	P	I	D
			A	L	E		A	S			
O	Y	S	T	E	R	S		S	T	R	A	P
V	E	E		R	E	V		E	G	O
A	T	T	I	C		A	E	R	O	S	O	L
			H	E		T	O	R			
S	O	C	I	A	L		A	A	R	G	H
I	C	E	C	R	E	A	M	C	O	N	E
T	A	N		T	E	D		L	O	A	N
E	S	T		H	R	S		E	F	T	S

#9

P	U	S	H		C	A	P	S
A	S	P	I	C		S	O	V	I	E	T
N	E	R	V	O	U	S	T	W	I	T	C	H
T	R	Y		C	R	E	E		D	A	T	E
			A	G	A	M					
P	A	L	A	C	E		R	I	S	P
E	R	A	T	O		C	U	T	I	E
R	E	P	E	L		T	U	N	D	R	A
		A	B	H	O	R				
F	E	L	T		A	U	R	A		C	P	U
B	R	E	A	T	H	H	I	T	C	H	E	S
I	N	V	E	N	T		E	R	A	S	E
	S	A	L	T			T	R	O	D	

#10

N	Y	C		E	R	R		B	O	A
O	A	R		T	O	O		E	O	N
S	W	O	O	N	W	O	R	T	H	Y
		C	H	A		T	H	E
O	D	I	U	M		C	E	L	L	O
E	R	N	S		P	A	R	A	S	O	L
R	O	C		S	E	G	O	S		A	D	O
O	U	T	C	R	O	P		A	M	I	R
P	R	O	O	F		F	E	Y	E	R
	P	R	E		I	O	N
F	R	E	N	C	H	B	R	E	A	D
O	A	K		T	O	E		I	D	O
P	Y	A		S	E	X		D	D	T

#11

Across/grid letters: SAY ESP VAR / CRAM ONTO IRA / AGRA GROT CIS / LUNG LOOP OOH / DESIREBLOOMS / ORE UNTO / SHIMS TREES / AURA TOR / FRENCHKISSED / HAT TORE ACNE / URL ICON KAVA / LIE CONS IDOL / ASS SAG SIS

#12

GAPS HAM NAME / ELAN IRA IDOL / LETOFFTHEHOOK / ORISON / HASTY GIANT / IDLY DEADSEA / VII INN PIG / ODYSSEY SAGE / SEOUL ECLAT / EOLITH / FIRSTDANCE FEE / OREO GUT MERE / PEST EDO EWER

#13

RAMP LOP SMOG / OBOE APE PANE / BOWLOVER UNIT / HEADFIRST / ATTAR EDGE / LOAM CYCLE / POP CRETE AAH / DUETO RIDE / HERD MELON / CABLETIES / GAZA NEONATAL / OVER CAT LOCI / TALK ERA EYED

#14

ODDS TAO WET / RAJA ALL AVOW / EDIT KID TIRO / BITE THATLIP / LONER AIL / BOUSES TRE PAN / OAT RUE / XFILES IDEATE / LEE NARCO / FREAKINGHOT / LEAN SEE DISH / UNTO MRS ECHO / BOSS SOT DEED

#15

CUFF JAR ARTS / OGEE ALA SOUP / ILLS BOT SAGA / FITTOBETIED / ARE ALT / OSTLER TESLAS / ROW EGO / BLONDE LEGION / ANC YEA / CRAZYINLOVE / HAIR EON ORAL / ICAO MUG SELL / MEOW ASS HOES

#16

O	P	P	E	D		L	I	T		M	A	D	E
A	R	E	A			E	T	E		A	N	O	N
F	O	R	G	I	V	E	M	E		K	I	S	S
		G	L	I	M	P	S	E					
A	C	K	E	E				P	U	P	A	S	
G	I	N	R	U	M	M	Y		P	E	S	T	
A	G	O		M	O	R	E	S		R	Y	E	
P	A	W	L		A	S	P	H	O	D	E	L	
E	R	N	I	E			A	C	U	T	E		
		E	R	A	S	U	R	E					
B	O	U	G	A	I	N	V	I	L	L	E	A	
E	A	S	E		D	I	E		L	E	A	K	
E	T	A	S		S	P	A		I	O	T	A	

#17

D	R	E	W		A	S	S		I	A	M	B
A	U	R	A		R	A	P		C	L	I	O
L	E	G	S	L	I	K	E	J	E	L	L	O
		P	E	D	I	C	A	B				
C	O	A	S	T			T	R	O	U	P	E
O	R	R		U	S	S	R		X	B	O	X
A	G	E		P	I	O	U	S		O	R	C
T	A	N	G		D	U	M	P		A	T	E
I	N	T	O	N	E		R	A	T	E	L	
			K	I	D	S	K	I	N			
R	O	Y	A	L	R	I	N	G	T	O	N	E
O	D	O	R		U	T	E		I	C	O	N
W	E	N	T		M	E	W		C	A	R	D

#18

A	C	E		A	L	P		S	A	V	E
D	U	M	A		B	A	A		C	L	E	G
Z	E	P	P	E	L	I	N		A	G	R	A
		I	S	M	Y	C	O	M	M	A	N	D
F	I	R	E	S			R	U	P	E	E	
A	T	E			O	C	A	S				
A	S	S		B	I	O	M	E		C	R	Y
			O	L	G	A			H	U	E	
	S	C	A	R	F			B	W	A	N	A
S	K	I	R	T	I	S	S	U	E	S		
M	A	G	I		R	E	P	R	I	S	A	L
E	T	A	S		E	R	R		R	I	C	E
W	E	R	E		D	A	Y		S	T	Y	

#19

S	O	D	A		O	R	B		T	A	N	H
O	V	A	L		F	I	R		O	D	O	R
H	A	L	L	O	F	M	I	R	R	O	R	S
			B	U	S	S	T	O	P			
O	C	C	U	R			C	L	O	T	S	
D	R	A	T		S	P	H	E	R	I	C	
D	I	N			T	I	E			N	O	N
M	O	S	A	I	C	S		P	E	R	E	
		P	E	A	R	L		P	I	A	N	O
			F	E	E	D	B	A	G			
B	L	U	E	S	T	E	E	L	P	O	U	T
B	E	L	L		T	A	N		E	R	S	E
C	I	T	Y		O	F	T		N	E	E	D

#20

W	O	O	S		C	O	Y		U	G	L	I
I	L	I	A		A	R	E		N	E	A	T
S	I	L	L		P	E	T		R	E	P	S
P	O	S	S	E	S	S	I	V	E			
			A	N	I			I	S	L	E	
H	A	M		E	C	S	T	A	T	I	C	
E	R	A		U	K	E			O	H	O	
I	L	L	U	M	I	N	E		N	O	R	
A	L	E	S			T	O	E				
			G	A	R	G	A	N	T	U	A	N
A	G	R	A		A	R	C		U	N	C	O
S	Y	N	C		S	O	L		D	I	N	G
S	P	A	Y		E	K	E		E	X	E	S

#21

```
O P A H . H O D . . V A M P
P A N E . A Y E . . A L O E
S L I P T H E C O L L A R .
. . C A N Z O N I . . . . .
U M I A K . . O S C A N . .
S E N T E N C E . E D D O .
A N C . N O R M A . R O E .
G U A M . S T U B B O R N .
E S S A Y . . A R M E D . .
. . R E J O I C E . . . . .
I F I M N O T T I E D U P .
S I L O . A T E . C O S H .
M E L T . N O M . H E E D .
```

#22

```
U S E . . G A S . S O R E
S E C T . A G O . T R O T
A C H E . T A M . E A C H
. S I L V E R B A L L S .
. . D I E . . R N A . . .
S A N C E R R E . E S S E
A L A . P E A R L . H O G
P I S A . S H O A L I N G
. . R O T . T I N . . . .
K I N K Y A S H E L L . .
M I N I . L Y E . G E A R
B L O C . E A R . E A S Y
A N N A . S H E . F E E .
```

#23

```
R A S P . E M U . P L E A
A L O E . V A N . R E N T
M I S S W E T B L O U S E
. . T I S S U E . . . . .
B E F O G . C A M E R A .
A R E . L E K . A L E S .
S I L T . O W L . D E M I
I C O N . W E E . M I D .
C A N T A B . E L I T E .
. . C R A G G Y . . . . .
C H E S T O F W O N D E R
P O E T . W R Y . C O M E
U G L Y . S O N . H E S S
```

#24

```
I K E . G M T . . B R A .
C A V I A . R A W . S E E N
E V E N . A L I . E N V Y .
D A R K K N I G H T . . . .
. L E D . S O A K S . . . .
S C R E A M S . W E N C H .
O H O . A I L . E A R . . .
S A T A N . B A S K E T S .
. T H R O B . W A R . . . .
. T R I P L E A X E L . . .
E G I S . L E E . A R I A .
G O R Y . G A S . L A R S .
O D E . E N S . Y E S . . .
```

#25

```
L E O . D I M . S L A B
A T M . A D O . P I L E
C H E S T E R F I E L D
. G L A M O U R . . . .
E S S A Y . C L E A R .
T H U S . D E C L A R E
C A M . N O W A Y . H A S
H A L O G E N . B A C H
S C O T T . B A T T Y .
. I C E B E R G . . . .
A N O T H E R W O M A N
S E R E . T I E . A G E
P E E R . H E R . N O W
```

#26

```
O D E S . G N U . S O W S
P O S Y . R A N . N O O K
E D A M . E R A . A H O Y
D O U B L E C R A P . . .
. . O A T . M I A S M .
I M P L Y . B E R T H A
T A U . S O D . A L B .
. C R U S T Y . R A M I E
E R R O R . S I R . . .
. . S T U C K O N H E R
D E L I . D O E . I O T A
E V E N . E K E . C O A T
C E D E . L E T . A P S E
```

#27

```
D A U B . O D D . S T E W
O K R A . W A R . T R A Y
S A N D . E M A C I A T E
. . G O N E W I L D . . .
C A M E L . . N A T I V E
O C A . L O B E . S T E P
R O D . A X I A L . I R E
G R A B . Y O R E . O D E
I N S E A M . S I N E S
. . H E D O N I S T . .
R H E T O R I C . C R O W
Y E L L . O N E . H Y P E
A X L E . N E D . Y E T I
```

#28

```
A U T O . H E R . V A L E
S L O P . O W E . A C I D
I N F O . R E V . L A V A
F A U R E S R E Q U I E M
. . T O E . R U E . . .
A L M O N D . B A D E G G
L A B . . . . . . D U E
I C A R U S . A T H O M E
. . U S A . P I E . . .
A N K L E B R A C E L E T
L O N E . R A T . H A T E
B E E R . A S H . A N N A
A L E S . S H Y . W E A R
```

#29

```
A W L S . J A B . R A Y
C H O C . E G O . V I L E
T A B U . W A G . O O P S
S M O L D E R I N G . . .
. . P O L . E T U D E .
O Y S T E R S . H E A R T
P I E . Y I P . C G I
S P R A G . S U R G E O N
. S A L E S . P E N . .
. . U L T R A S O U N D
D O R M . R A T . S T A Y
E V E S . A T E . E A S E
W A D . P A S . S H A D
```

#30

```
T B A R . D D T . B I N G
U R G E . E R R . I C O N
G I R L . L I E . T A R P
. G A Y Q U E S T I O N .
. . O D D S O N . . .
C A N A P E . . G A L A
B R O T H S . C U L L E T
S E N T . A S Y L U M
. . A I R E R S . . .
D I C T A T O R I A L
H U S H . Y U M . D O I N
I D L E . O D E . O N T O
S E E D . N E D . L E E R
```

#31

```
G A G A . L O B . U G L I
A G E S . E R R . N E A T
B A T H R O B E B E L T S
. . B U N . T E A . . . .
A M A I N . H A S T E . .
D A R N . H U R R Y U P .
O N E . D O Z E D . T O P
. I N S U L I N . C O X A
. C A P R I . B E R Y L .
. . A S S . F U N . . . .
I D O N T T R U S T H I M
C O C K . I N N . E U R O
Y E A S . C A D . R E E D
```

#32

```
S P E C . E L F . R A W
H I G H . B U R . C I A O
A S I A . O N E . A C H E
M A S K I N G T A P E . .
. . R L Y . S I R . . . .
A L G A E . G A L I L E O
W E I . M A W . E R R . .
N O N S T O P . O S I E R
. O I L . D A Y . . . . .
. B U T T E R F L I E S .
L I O N . E R A . V O L T
A C I D . R I M . A W A Y
B E L . S E A . S A N E .
```

#33

```
S C A M . D A D . L O T
A O N E . A C E . D E L I
R I O T . Y A P . P O D S
I N N E R B I T C H . . .
. . . O N O . H A I R R Y
P H A R A O H . B L O O D
A I D . K A Y . C G I . .
S N A R . F . J E T S K I S
D R A B . S . L E U . . .
. . . L I T T L E B L I P
F O A L . O B I . O U S E
D U L Y . N A N . R A N G
A R E . E R G . N U T S
```

#34

```
W I M P . D I E . B L E W
A R E A . R A Y . E I R E
N E A P . E M E R G E N T
. . L A C Y B R I E F S .
I D Y L L . . H O T . . .
D U B . A C H Y . S T U B
E M U . N A O M I . A G A
S A G A . R E E D . P L Y
. . M E N . O A S I S . .
P A R K I N G L O T . . .
M E D I E V A L . R E N T
B R A T . A V E . T R I O
A U R A . L Y E . A S H Y
```

#35

```
B A S T . E M S . B A L I
E C H O . B E T . E X A M
C H O U . O N E . C O U P
K E E P Y O U R H A N D S
. . . E E K . E E L . . .
S C R E W S . O R M O L U
E O N . . . . . . W A S .
C L A M P S . E V I N C E
. . E R E . T I T . . . .
F O R G O T T H E S H O T
A G A R . T H Y . E E R Y
Y E T I . E E N . L E E K
S E E M . E Y E . F L O E
```

#36

A	D	D	A	M		M	A	T		S	W	A	Y
W	A	R	E		I	C	Y		L	A	N	E	
O	T	I	C		R	A	P	P	O	R	T	S	
L	A	S	C	I	V	I	O	U	S				
	T	A	R		R	H	I	N	O				
C	O	O		A	F	O	U	L		L	A	P	
O	P	T		L	I	T		L	I	E			
S	A	L		R	U	L	E	R		O	L	D	
T	H	E	T	A		Y	A	M					
	A	C	L	O	S	E	R	E	I	N			
I	N	C	R	E	A	S	E		I	N	D	O	
N	O	G	O		I	L	L		S	E	E	R	
K	N	I	T		C	O	L		E	D	A	M	

#37

O	T	T	O		B	U	S		V	E	E	R
P	U	R	L		A	R	E		E	R	G	O
E	N	I	D		B	A	D	I	N	A	G	E
C	A	P	I	T	U	L	A	T	E			
	P	E	A		T	S	E	T	S	E		
C	U	E		L	O	G	E		R	A	T	S
O	L	D		C	R	O	S	S	S		L	O	P
O	N	U	S		D	O	T	E		L	A	Y
P	A	P	U	A	N		R	H	O			
	B	L	A	C	K	B	E	R	R	Y		
T	E	R	M	I	N	A	L		I	D	E	A
E	T	U	I		C	P	A		N	E	A	P
C	A	N	T		E	O	N		E	R	R	S

#38

A	N	T	I		D	A	B		B	L	A	H
L	O	A	D		A	G	A		R	I	P	E
A	R	M	A	G	N	A	C		U	S	E	R
		H	E	A	R	K	E	N				
C	A	R	O	L		D	R	E	A	D		
E	R	A		D	E	R	R	I	E	R	E	
N	I	B		L	A	G	O	S		G	O	T
T	A	B	L	E	T	O	P		I	O	N	
	S	I	E	V	E		T	E	S	L	A	
		C	A	L	O	R	I	E				
R	A	P	T		I	C	E	C	R	E	A	M
A	L	T	O		N	A	N		I	N	T	O
W	E	A	R		E	S	T		E	D	E	N

#39

O	A	T		O	D	O		O	P	T
P	I	A		O	U	R		D	O	E
S	T	R	A	P	P	E	D	M	E	I	N
		S	E	S	S	I	O	N		
L	A	S	E	R		N	I	S	E	I
A	P	E	R		W	E	A	R	E	R	S
M	N	O		C	R	O	R	E		R	A	P
E	U	P	H	O	N	Y		R	O	A	R
A	L	L	I	N		M	E	R	C	Y
	A	N	G	E	L	I	C			
O	U	T	O	F	C	O	N	T	R	O	L
O	F	T		U	R	N		O	I	L	Y
H	O	E		L	U	G		O	D	E

#40

S	H	A	H		I	V	Y		A	N	N	A
H	E	R	O		S	E	E		L	O	O	N
A	L	I	T		R	N	A		E	N	V	Y
G	L	A	D	I	A	T	R	I	X			
		O	N	E		N	O	I	S	E		
W	R	I	G	G	L	E		N	A	A	N	
E	E	C		I	T	S		R	I	M		
T	A	B	U		C	O	N	F	I	D	E
D	O	U	S	E		R	I	O			
	N	A	M	E	C	H	A	N	G	E	
P	E	C	K		B	Y	E		M	A	R	E
U	R	G	E		E	E	R		E	M	I	R
P	A	I	R		D	R	Y		D	E	N	Y

99 Shades of Play

#41

```
S A E _ A L L _ S E A
A I L _ V I I _ P E P
C R E M E B R U L E E
_ _ M A S S A G E _ _
S T A I R _ H E R S _
N A M _ C H A R _ N E A R _ R
A B O _ S U G A R _ B R O
P O U R _ M O T E _ E G O
O R E O _ I S L E T
C O N S E N T
T O O H A N D S O M E
E R R _ B I D _ V O W
L E D _ S T Y _ E N E
```

#42

```
S T A B _ T O R _ B A L E
W I L E _ A R E _ I D E S
A T O M _ R E D _ C E N T
G O T O U T O F H A N D
_ _ A K A _ O U R
D O W N E R _ X E B E C S
O N E _ M B A
C O B W E B _ P R I S S Y
O D E _ A I M
B L O O D P U M P I N G
G O O D _ L I P _ A R E A
U R G E _ A T E _ L O A M
N E E D _ M A R _ A N T E
```

#43

```
T A P S _ R O D _ L U T E
A R E A _ A L E _ I P A D
P A L M _ C I L A N T R O
B L O W Y O U R T O P
M A R _ S E E
S C E N A R I O _ L A M A
O I L _ P U R R S _ L O P
U G L Y _ S K Y P I L O T
E A T _ A T E
S E A R I N G R A G E
H O L S T E I N _ L O G E
E A S T _ S P A _ I R I S
P R E Y _ T A T _ C Y S T
```

#44

```
M I L E _ M A D _ L A O S
A V E R _ A B A _ I N F O
O Y E R _ G U N S M I T H
A G I T A T E
S P A T E _ U N L I T
C A T A M A R A N _ A L A
O R E _ D U N _ N I B
U S A _ L O N D O N C A B
T E M P O _ S E E D Y
S U B C L U B
S T E A D I L Y _ U N D O
H E A L _ T U N _ L O O P
H A R M _ S E X _ A B E T
```

#45

```
D E L I _ A S P _ B O L A
O P E D _ L E I _ R U E S
C I T E _ O R C H A R D S
C H A S T E K I S S
A S H _ I T S
M A R _ E B O N _ Y E G G
E G G _ D O D G E _ N E E
G O Y A _ M E S A _ V E T
D E B _ S U E
Y E S S E A T T L E
S K E P T I C S _ T O W N
H E A T _ T H E _ E P E E
E A R S _ E T A _ R E S T
```

Solutions

#46

```
W A K E   M O N   H O D S
A C E R   E T A   E X I T
L A M A   R I P   L E V Y
L I P S T I C K L I N E
      E A T   I O U
C I T R U S   N Y M P H O
I R E       R O C
S A L A M I   A D V E N T
    N U T   S U E
  B R I G H T Y E L L O W
S L A M   A I L   L O V E
H U L A   C P U   U S E R
H E E L   A I M   M E R E
```

#47

```
L U S T   S A T   S E R I E
E T U I   U F O   A M O K
D E B S   I R E   T U N E
      D A Y T O D A Y
T H I N E     W R A P
S E V E N T E E N   D E N
A L I   A R P   M A O
R O D   H I S S Y   F I T S
    T E A M   A R T S Y
    S M A S H H I T
H A S T   L E A   N I S I
A C H E   M R S   G N A T
J E E R   S A P   E G G S
```

#48

```
A T O P   H E S   G A S P
M A R L   Y A K   O D O R
P I C A   P R I M R O S E
    A S P E N T R I P
    H I   T S E T S E
H I C   P A V E   R I O T
A L E   S M I R K   V A N
R I L L   B A S E   E R A
M A L A W I   P I
    U N H E E D I N G
W A L K O N B Y   D U P E
O R A L   C O N   I T E M
E E R Y   E N E   E S A U
```

#49

```
Y O R E   N B C   G N P
O W E N   A L A   A I L
U N B E L I E V A B L Y
      A V A I L
    L E V E R A G E S
H E A L   R I O T E R
I M P O S T   E N S I L E
S U P P L E   I N K S
    S E A S O N I N G
      S T R A D
R E D H U L A S   K I R T
A R E   D O N   I R O N
M E N   O P S   N E W T
```

#50

```
P R O F   H I P   T R A Y
H A L L   O N O   H Y P E
I N D E C E N T   E A R N
    N U R S E R Y
O B E S E   N A R C O
U R G E   H I C K E Y S
T A R   L E V E E   C A B
  S E N O R E S   H A K A
  S T E L E   C E D A R
    C L U B C A R
A B E T   P R O P O S A L
S O M A   O A T   I O T A
H O U R   N E E   N U M B
```

99 Shades of Play

#51

H	A	T	S		R	E	S		M	E	A	D

Row 1: HATS / RES / MEAD
Row 2: AGHA / APT / OSLO
Row 3: SOUVENIR / NAME
Row 4: RIDICULOUS
Row 5: CHINO / TEC
Row 6: REF / CATALPA
Row 7: YLEM / OWE / EONS
Row 8: PROSPER / TIP
Row 9: SOY / FUSSY
Row 10: COQUETTISH
Row 11: GURU / DISRAELI
Row 12: ESSE / IRA / GRIN
Row 13: EPOS / TOR / EDEN

#52

Row 1: SHOW / ELF / TILL
Row 2: AURA / NEO / IDEA
Row 3: WHEREVER / PLAY
Row 4: COY / LAPEL
Row 5: SPURN / ODE
Row 6: ORGY / PROTEM
Row 7: POL / URN / SEN
Row 8: WILLGO / EASE
Row 9: YEA / SQUAW
Row 10: ARSON / YOU
Row 11: THAI / DAEDALUS
Row 12: HORN / ALL / TOSH
Row 13: EYES / NIP / EPEE

#53

Row 1: CUSP / OCT / OTIC
Row 2: OVER / PRY / CANE
Row 3: DELI / EAR / TBSP
Row 4: SALMONBAGEL
Row 5: ARE / NOTED
Row 6: WHALER / TASTY
Row 7: EEL / ONO
Row 8: LHASA / DAPPER
Row 9: MADAM / ILL
Row 10: MRMEGABUCKS
Row 11: AMBO / BUD / COHO
Row 12: SARI / ALE / KLAN
Row 13: SPAT / ELM / YANG

#54

Row 1: BAT / GOD / TWO
Row 2: AGRA / EGO / JOIN
Row 3: KIEV / NEW / UNTO
Row 4: UNFETTERED
Row 5: RUE / YEAS
Row 6: WRITTEN / CHAIN
Row 7: EON / LIP / LEO
Row 8: TOTUP / PEPPERS
Row 9: DORSA / ROE
Row 10: BITCHTROLL
Row 11: PAPA / BOA / CLUE
Row 12: EARN / AMP / HIKE
Row 13: WHO / YES / OER

#55

Row 1: DIAS / LIT / EDAM
Row 2: IOWA / ADO / CAGE
Row 3: PUNCHMYPILLOW
Row 4: REPLICA
Row 5: ARGAL / ETHIC
Row 6: DALLIERS / SODA
Row 7: ODE / ORIEL / MIN
Row 8: PINK / ROTATION
Row 9: TINEA / THETA
Row 10: TAFFETA
Row 11: BATTHEEYELIDS
Row 12: EVIL / TEA / IDEA
Row 13: GENE / ASS / AONE

#56

S	C	O	T		C	B	S		W	A	D	D
O	P	A	H		I	R	A		I	L	I	A
S	A	R	I		G	I	G	G	L	I	N	G
		R	O	S	E	O	I	L				
F	I	R	S	T		N	I	C	A	D		
I	N	I	T	I	A	L	S		S	O	L	I
B	U	G		S	P	O	K	E		R	I	D
E	R	I	N		T	W	I	N	I	N	G	S
R	E	D	I	D			V	A	U	N	T	
		T	O	P	O	N	Y	M				
D	R	Y	W	H	I	T	E		B	A	K	U
V	I	I	I		T	I	S		I	R	I	S
D	O	N	T		A	C	T		C	E	D	E

#57

M	A	A	M		C	P	U		L	A	M	A
A	L	S	O		H	A	T		A	M	E	N
O	B	I	T		U	S	A		N	O	S	Y
		A	F	T	E	R	S	H	O	C	K	S
			O	W	N		A	R	E			
E	G	I	S	E	S		N	E	T	T	L	E
R	A	T								A	I	R
A	S	S	E	T	S		C	O	P	P	E	R
			L	E	A		A	W	L			
	F	I	V	E	M	I	L	L	I	O	N	
S	A	R	I		O	B	I		E	V	E	N
A	V	I	S		S	I	C		R	A	V	E
M	E	S	H		A	D	O		S	L	E	W

#58

A	S	A	P		H	A	H		K	A	R	T
F	A	I	R		O	V	A		I	C	O	N
T	Y	R	O		P	E	N	I	T	E	N	T
			W	E	I	R	D	O	S			
S	C	O	L	D			Y	U	C	C	A	S
O	R	R		I	M	A	M		H	O	V	E
D	A	B		T	I	D	A	L		R	A	N
O	V	E	R		N	O	N	O		A	I	D
M	E	D	U	S	A		B	E	L	L	S	
		N	O	T	A	T	E	S				
M	A	N	W	H	O	R	E		S	O	U	L
A	R	E	A		R	I	M		A	C	R	E
D	E	W	Y		Y	A	P		Y	A	N	K

#59

L	O	A	F		L	O	T		S	E	T	A
A	I	N	U		O	N	O		C	R	O	P
B	L	I	S	S	F	U	L		R	A	P	T
		S	A	T	S	U	M	A				
A	L	K	Y	D			O	P	U	S		
S	I	R		V	A	R	I	E	T	Y		
S	P	A		L	E	G	A	L		E	R	E
	P	A	R	A	G	O	N		R	I	O	
Y	L	E	M		A	V	I	A	N			
		M	A	E	S	T	R	O				
S	A	G	O		P	L	A	T	I	N	U	M
K	I	E	V		I	O	N		D	O	S	E
I	D	L	E		C	B	S		S	W	A	T

#60

E	L	F		O	A	R		F	U	L	L
L	E	A		A	C	E		O	R	E	O
M	I	L	E	H	I	G	H	C	L	U	B
		S	T	U	D	I	O	S			
A	D	I	E	U		M	E	L	L	O	W
M	U	D		I	S	L	E		E	A	S	E
E	K	E		S	W	A	N	S		T	I	E
B	E	A	M		I	N	T	O		E	E	K
A	S	S	E	R	T			B	U	R	R	S
		D	U	C	H	I	E	S			
P	E	E	L	T	H	E	D	R	E	S	S
O	G	L	E		O	R	E		U	T	E
P	O	K	Y		N	O	S		P	Y	A

99 Shades of Play

#61

A	S	A	P		H	I	C		M	U	O	N
M	E	G	A		O	V	A		I	S	L	E
A	M	O	S		G	A	M		L	A	D	E
H	I	G	H	H	A	N	D	E	D			
			T	E	N		E	V	E	R	T	
A	B	H	O	R	S		N	E	W	E	R	
T	A	U				T	A	I				
	A	R	D	O	R		A	B	B	E	Y	S
S	T	A	R	E		G	A	Y				
	B	R	U	S	H	T	E	E	T	H		
N	U	M	B		B	O	A		B	R	I	O
O	R	A	L		E	M	S		Y	A	P	S
S	L	O	E		N	E	T		E	S	S	E

#62

E	T	A	S		F	I	T		C	B	S
P	E	R	T		E	R	A		S	L	U	E
A	R	C	O		T	O	P		C	U	R	E
P	H	I	L	A	N	D	E	R	E	R	
	I	C	E		A	N	A				
L	A	V		A	M	E	N	D	M	E	N	T
A	G	A		A	R	C		N	E	E	
B	O	L	L	I	N	G	E	R		D	O	N
	I	M	P		O	V	A				
	S	U	F	F	O	C	A	T	I	N	G
M	U	S	E		W	H	O		A	G	A	R
P	E	E	R		E	O	N		N	E	V	E
H	R	S		R	U	E		D	R	E	G

#63

O	H	M		I	C	Y		P	E	R
P	O	I		L	O	O	M		A	W	E
T	R	A	I	L	S	K	I	S	S	E	S
S	N	O	B		H	E	R	O			
	W	I	T		L	I	M	B	O		
O	P	O	S	S	U	M		N	A	A	N	S
N	U	T		G	A	S		T	E	A	
O	R	I	E	L		O	P	P	R	E	S	S
E	S	T	E	R		Y	O	U			
	A	G	E	D		E	N	D	S		
N	U	T	S	A	B	O	U	T	Y	O	U
A	S	H		L	U	S	T		O	D	E
N	A	Y		T	E	E		N	O	T

#64

S	P	Y		D	E	N		P	O	I
A	Y	E		E	R	A		A	I	D	S
C	A	S	T	A	S	P	E	L	L	O	N
			E	R	E		A	V	E	R	T
M	A	Y	H	E	M		O	R	E		
E	L	A	I	N	E		K	N	O	L	L	S
N	E	R	D			L	I	E	U		
S	E	N	E	C	A		S	C	A	R	E	D
		O	H	M		H	A	R	A	S	S
P	A	P	U	A		E	E	L			
O	N	E	T	R	A	C	K	M	I	N	D
E	T	A	S		S	H	E		T	O	R
M	E	T		S	O	L		T	R	Y

#65

J	A	M	B		F	E	W		D	U	D	E
O	V	E	R		I	C	E		I	R	O	N
B	E	T	A		S	H	A	C	K	L	E	S
			N	E	T	T	L	E	D			
H	A	R	D	Y			P	I	T	A	S	
A	B	A	T	A	B	L	E		K	O	L	A
N	O	D		S	L	Y	L	Y		E	A	T
G	R	A	M		T	E	M	E	R	I	T	Y
S	T	R	A	P			T	O	N	E	R	
			T	A	K	E	A	I	M			
D	A	Z	Z	L	I	N	G		P	U	M	A
I	C	A	O		L	I	E		E	S	P	Y
P	E	P	S		O	D	D		R	A	G	E

#66

```
S H I N   S I M   K I T
I O T A   W O O   I R A
R E D S P I N N A K E R
    A U G   G N U
S M E L T   R O Y A L
P O X   D E M U R E
A C T   S A D L Y   R A M
  H O B A R T   A V E
  A L I B I   D O Y E N
    A L A   Y O U
M I X E D S I G N A L S
O V A   N A P   C L A P
T E L   E N S   E L M Y
```

#67

```
H A I R   H E D   T I S
A N T E   E T U I   I R K
M A S C A R A E D   D A Y
      O L D S T Y L E
G R O U P     L E W D
L A P P   B I L L I A R D
O D E   A R I A S   T I E
P A R A N O I D   S E L F
  R E I N     C U R L Y
  T R A D E G A P
E S T   L O V E B I T E S
B O A   S T E M   N U L L
B U S   E N S   E M M Y
```

#68

```
I D S   S H A F T   E T A
C O O   L A V E R   L A B
E D O   E L E M I   A L L
D O N T D O R O M A N C E
    A G E   R E P
O O D L E S   A R R A N T
V A I L       I D E A
A R G Y L E   F R O Z E N
    H A Y   E E R
C R O O K E D S M I L E S
R O M   E L I T E   E V E
U S E   R E D E D   V I E
D E N   S T O R Y   A L P
```

#69

```
S P E D   R I B   M E N S
U R S A   E R R   I D O L
M I S C   M O O   N I N A
  G E T T I N G O N T O P
    Y E N   A D O
B A W L E D   N E W B I E
E N E       I L K
L I B I D O   B A B B L E
    S O P   A G E
U N D O N E T O O F A R
F O A M   N A B   A R E A
O N C E   E R A   L I D S
S E E R   R O B   L A O S
```

#70

```
M E N U   R A T   P R O
U R A L   E T H   S E A R
S N I T   F O E   C A N E
H E L I C O P T E R
    M A R   A D A G E
E X D O M M E   O M E G A
E M U   S L Y   N I L
C A P O N   M A L T E S E
  S E P I A   C A R
    T H I G H H I G H S
M A G I   D O T   P I O N
B L O C   E Y E   U G L I
A P T   D A D   P O M P
```

217

#71

T	E	A	M		T	H	E		C	E	P
A	B	L	E		H	I	L	T	A	R	E
U	B	E	R	B	O	S	S	Y	N	A	N
	M	O	U	S	E	P	A	D			
U	N	S	A	Y		I	S	L	E		
S	A	W	N		B	L	U	S	H	E	S
A	C	E		W	R	I	S	T	P	S	I
R	E	S	H	A	P	E		S	I	A	L
E	T	U	I			V	I	N	Y	L	
	P	E	R	S	O	N	A	E			
E	Y	E		R	O	P	E	T	R	I	C	K
T	E	A		S	L	E	W		R	O	U	E
H	A	S			D	D	T		A	U	R	A

#72

N	E	W	E	L		R	A	Y	O	N
I	R	O	N	I	C		A	D	O	B	E
P	R	E	S	S	H	I	S	S	U	I	T
			A	R	C						
L	I	M	O		S	K	A	L	A	D
A	N	O	M	I	E		L	E	A	G	U	E
W	A	X	E	D		A	B	A	C	A
S	P	I	G	O	T		B	R	E	V	E	T
	T	E	A		A	H	A		L	E	S	S
			N	U	B						
T	R	A	C	K	H	E	R	C	E	L	L
E	N	D	U	E		L	E	A	V	E	S
G	A	Z	E	R		F	R	E	U	D

#73

F	L	A	P		F	C	C		I	N	T	O
B	E	T	A		A	H	A		N	O	I	R
I	A	M	N	O	T	A	N	A	S	S	E	T
			D	I	S	T	A	N	T			
N	A	T	A	L		P	I	E	C	E
A	L	A	S		T	E	M	P	L	E
B	I	B		A	B	A	S	E		O	R	B
	G	O	B	L	I	N		G	A	I	A
N	O	R	I	A			I	R	K	E	D
		A	B	S	E	N	C	E			
H	A	D	H	I	S	W	A	Y	W	I	T	H
O	V	U	M		E	E	R		U	R	S	A
W	E	D	S		D	R	Y		P	E	P	S

#74

G	R	A	M	P		T	A	N	E	R	D
A	I	N	U		R	U	N		O	V	E	R
N	A	N	S		O	F	T		V	E	D	A
G	L	A	S	W	A	L	L		R	O	W
		E	E	L		E	A	S	Y
B	O	U	L	E	S		R	H	O	D	E	S
O	W	N			A	R	K
A	L	K	A	L	I	C	L	A	Y	E	Y
		I	N	O	N		A	I	R
M	A	N		B	A	L	L	S	R	O	O	M
U	R	D	U		N	I	L		E	R	G	O
S	E	L	F		E	M	U		S	E	L	L
K	A	Y	O		R	E	S		T	O	E	D

#75

M	A	D		H	M	M		Y	A	R
A	G	E		C	I	A	O		E	S	P
R	A	P		U	L	T	R	A	T	A	M
C	R	A	C	K	T	H	E	W	H	I	P
		R	U	E		L	E	I
R	E	T	D		S	A	L	C	H	A	R
O	R	E		A	B	O	E	G	O
C	E	D	E		P	A	S	P	R	O	D
		M	O	P		I	R	E
M	O	U	T	H	T	O	M	O	U	T	H
M	A	O		T	I	A	R	A	P	A	Y
A	D	Z		R	E	A	M	O	L	D
T	E	E		E	L	L		N	E	E

#76

```
S O A R . A S P . . S E T
E D G E . M O O . M I R O
T O R C . E L L . O R E O
T R A I L B I K E S . . .
. . . P T A . A T E U P .
B O X E R S . S A Y S O .
Y A M . . . . . S K I . .
H A R P S . G A R R E T .
U S U A L . U S E . . . .
. . . F L Y F I S H I N G
S U R F . E E L . A L O E
A R E S . S A T . S I L L
E N D . . T R Y . H A L T
```

#77

```
O P A L . B A D . E C H O
R O T E . O D E . R A I N
B L O G . L A M B A S T E
. S M A R T M O U T H . .
. . . T A I . . D O C S .
B O L O G N A . . R E B .
O N O . A G A P E . O R E
A I D . . H E L I P A D .
. T E R N . A L B . . . .
. . S U B M I S S I O N .
R E T I C U L A . D H A L
I R A N . T I N . E I R E
B A R S . T A T . M O C K
```

#78

```
S L E D . T O G . . P T A
M A D E . O R E . P E A S
E V I L . Y E N . O A T H
W A T E R W O R K S . . .
. . . T A I . E A S E L .
A L D E N T E . Y E M E N
D U O . H E R . . I V Y .
S C O L D . K I N E T I C
. K R A A L . D A M . . .
. . B L O N D G I A N T .
O B O E . S O L . G R A Y
H U L L . E V E . R I N K
O D D . . R A D . E A S E
```

#79

```
E R G O . L A C . B A A L
G O E R . E M U . A L S O
G E T A R O O M . D E P T
. . C E N S U R E . . . .
S C A L D . L E G A L . .
O O Z E . H U N G R Y . .
T N T . W A I S T . O R E
. D E T E R S . A S I F .
O C E A N . E R E C T . .
. A L I B A B A . . . . .
E W E R . C L U B B I N G
T H R U . A I R . L O O P
C O R P . S P A . E U R O
```

#80

```
M I S C . B R A . R H O .
A R I A . L A G . F O N .
M A R R Y I N H A S T E .
. . . P E P . A G E . . .
A T S E A . . A N G R Y .
T A L L T A L E . T H O U
O B I . S T E N O . O A R
L O N G . M I S T R U S T
L O G O S . . T I L T S .
. . S E E . W E D . . . .
N I P A N E A R L O B E .
E R E . I T S . E V E N .
E E L . D A H . Y A L E .
```

99 Shades of Play

#81

ABEL · SPA · BLIP
SAXE · EEL · RENO
PACE · CAFFEINE
ICYSTARE
KASHA · LOCALE
EVE · CLEF · HUED
BIT · KARAT · TAG
ASAP · WASH · OVA
BOXERS · EMMER
LEUKEMIA
BROODING · ATOM
RIOT · TOG · MINE
AGHA · STY · ICON

#82

THUD · CBS · PAT
HATE · OUT · BODE
USAF · ERA · LION
SPHINXLIKE
LEI · READS
TELEOST · ARIA
OVA · TUT · SKI
EVES · BITCHIN
NADIR · EAR
GRANDPIANO
ABLE · NEO · SNUB
VEER · GAW · INFO
EGG · ERN · SAFE

#83

LAC · LEV · GEL
AGO · III · RAY
MASTERSUITE
TRUEING
BIALY · TIRADE
EDDY · PLATINUM
NIL · TRINE · NEB
NOISIEST · CUTE
EMBALM · DOLOR
FLOTSAM
EYESLOCKING
EEL · ADO · COO
NAY · ROT · STY

#84

ZONES · BBC · HAY
EVADE · RAY · EVE
RESIN · ARC · TEA
ONATIGHTLEASH
OHM · ERE
EAR · RES · ARI
BROWSE · RESALE
BASH · NOS · ELK
EEL · OTT
GETTINGCHEEKY
OPT · MOO · EYRIE
BEE · EGO · TESTA
YES · NOD · ESTER

#85

AWAY · CWT
MACAU · ALLIED
PIERS · LEAKED
FREAKY · SADIST
ROOF
GREMLIN · LATTE
PAYEES · VELOUR
OMEGA · DETENTE
PANE
BLINDPASSION
AENEAS · UTTER
REDEYE · METRO
ROD · MODE

#86

- TOMB · REV · BAA
- AVER · APE · GILL
- LAMA · TEN · ROOM
- CLENCHED FISTS
- DOE · ODE
- ABATOR · RAGTAG
- ROT · ALE
- MAMMEE · PEDDLE
- OWN · ERR
- SILVER GRAY · TIE
- ACAI · OHM · IOTA
- LOVE · LEI · COLT
- ENE · LET · ELLS

#87

- PRIG · RIO · TAMP
- AURA · ADD · ERIE
- CLAN · TOE · CEDE
- TENDRIL OF HAIR
- HAN · NAN
- BAAING · STOOLS
- ITS · NEE
- BEHALF · BAGOUT
- PAL · USA
- GIGAWATTS · MILE
- LOUT · NIL · BOIL
- UTAH · GEE · OWNS
- GAMY · ERR · LAKE

#88

- CLAP · SKI · CAPS
- HAIR · KIN · OLIO
- ADMIRE THE VIEW
- MEW · ALE
- ELVES · LINGO
- VII · JETSET
- EMS · SPORE · ETA
- BOYTOY · KEG
- OREOS · BASRA
- SIT · SUM
- TWITCHING PALM
- WADE · OVA · LIEU
- ODOR · CEP · YLEM

#89

- AQUA · BIT · CHUB
- DUNS · ERE · RARE
- ZITS · DON · ORGY
- TOO HANDSOME
- RUM · EEK
- LISTEN · RASPED
- ARK · TEA
- WEIRDO · THRALL
- AIR · SAE
- GIVE IT UP NOW
- SIDE · OER · TBAR
- EVEN · LEI · AONE
- TESS · EMS · LEES

#90

- AMPS · INS · BLAH
- LOAN · LEU · RILE
- POSITION PAPER
- PEA · DEN
- WOMEN · RADAR
- ADOS · TRESTLE
- NOT · TEASE · ONO
- REPASTS · THAT
- STRUT · DEALT
- OPT · TOE
- TIE ME UP SCOTTY
- SOAP · BAA · FINE
- PUTT · ERR · FETA

#91

```
D R A B   P A W     O B I T
R A N I   O C A     P A R A
A G O G   O A R     E G A D
T A N T A L I Z I N G
      O D E   O R E A D
A R C E D   E N E R G Y
M A O   U S E   E E N
  S A D I S T   M I S D O
  P L A N E   C O N
    M I N D B L O W I N G
G R I N   C O Y   A L O E
P I N T   A N D   R I S E
O B E Y   R Y E   D A Y S
```

#92

```
C U R D   S H H     R A F T
O G E E   T O O     E M I R
P L E A   E O N     C I T Y
E I F F E L T O W E R
      T E A   R O D
C A J O L E   S K E T C H
A N A         E G O
R I B A L D   C A T N I P
        F E Y   A L E
    D R U N K D I A L E D
F L E A   A I D   P A R A
D E E M   S L I   O D O R
A I D E   T O E   T E S T
```

#93

```
A S S     P E A     P A N
S K A     L A C     R I O
K I L L E R H E E L S
    T E A L E A F
L I B Y A     R A G E S
A L E     F I R E B R A T
T I N   A R M E D   A G E
H A N D S O F F   I R E
I D E A S     E U L E R
    R E P A C K S
B U T T S Q U E E Z E
E R E   S U E   R A T
E N D   T A D   S P A
```

#94

```
A P T   E T A   T E A
I R E   F A Q   A L P
D O N T T O U C H M E
  B O O S   A L I
S P O R T   N O N E S
P A S   S T A M I N A
A N C   S T O U P   T U G
D I S P O R T   O C A
A S T I R   C R U E L
  U T E   D O E R
C R A Z Y W I T H A K
F A R   E E K   A G E
C W T   D I E   B E G
```

#95

```
E M S   S I C   S Y N C
R A H   A D O   P O O R
G R E E K Y O G H U R T
    E V I L E Y E
S A C R A   E P R I N T
N D A   D E L I   E S A U
O D D   E V E N T   L I B
O T I S   E D G E   E R A
P O S E U R   N A T A L
    P S Y C H O S
C A R T E B L A N C H E
O B O E   I I I   O U T
W A T T   T O R   T E A
```

#96

```
E A S T . S P A . S W A P
E C H O . L E T . T O P E
L A I R . A R T . A V E R
. I N S A T I A B L E . .
. . O N E . I R K . . . .
F E I S T Y . N A S A L S
A W N . . . . . . B A P .
T E N R E C . B L O O D Y
. . U R L . Y E A . . . .
. S T R A W B E R R Y . .
G A I T . S O L . I A M B
A I D E . P R O . N I C E
B R E D . S E W . G N A T
```

#97

```
. A S H . O P S . S E A .
. D O E . L E A . A L P .
. D U R B E R V I L L E .
. . . M A O . O C A . . .
C H O I R S . R E M O T E
L I N T . . O E D I P U S
A L I . . C A D . E N S .
S A C K B U T . A R I A .
P R E N U P . P I R A C Y
. . O R R . A N C . . . .
. G E T T I N G I T O N .
N E T . T O E . A V E . .
P L Y . E R R . N A B . .
```

#98

```
S C A B . W A D . . L A .
C O L A . I R E . M E N U
A M E N . N A B . O D D S
M A S K E D B A L L . . .
. . E R R . R U D D Y . .
P H A R A O H . G Y R O .
I O N . W E E . A K A . .
. P O E T . S M I T T E N
. I N D I A . A D O . . .
. . U P T O N . G O O D .
S Y N C . O V A . G R A Y
H E B E . N E T . L A R K
E T C . E N E . E L S E .
```

#99

```
A R E A . C R T . P H I .
D A R N . H O O K . H A S
S P A G H E T T I . O H M
. . L A N C E L O T . . .
T O T E M . . T R O T . .
U S E R . B E W I T C H .
T I E . P A Y E E . E R R
. E N C A G E D . G L E E
. R A I N . C E L E B . .
. . G A D A B O U T . . .
A W E . A R A B E S Q U E
C A R . S A K I . B U R R
E N S . B E T . Y A L E .
```

ABOUT THE AUTHOR:

Myles Mellor is one of the most successful and prolific puzzle writers. He publishes over 100 puzzles per month all over the world and his puzzles have appeared in more than 600 magazines, newspapers, and Web sites. He recently published his 10,000th crossword puzzle. Visit his Web sites: ilovecrosswords. com and themecrosswords.com.